•THE 4th LIST
•OF SHIT
•THAT MADE
•ME A
•FEMINIST

Farida D.

Farida D. is an Arab gender researcher and poet, studying Arab women's everyday oppressions for over a decade. Through the process- she broke up with her hijab, set her high heels on fire, and authored a series of books. Farida's words have been on BBC Radio London, are continuously amplified by celebrities, and strolling all over social media. Contact her via email farida-d@outlook.com, or on Instagram @farida.d.author

BLACK

LIVES

MATTER.

To the rage;
where there is fire,
there can be fireworks too.

601.

He loves me
like a lullaby.

Pitter patter
butterfly.

Linear
familiar
fairytale.

Sunshine
no shadows.

The tiptoes
of my feet,
echoes
the melody
of his heartbeat.

His arms
fill my sky.

Open
broad.

We're on
the same road.

He loves me...
like nobody,
else.

He loves me...
the way I love,
myself.

602.

I was looking for you
for a long time,
in the eyes of men, built of heaven
but who never appreciated mine.

I had to go through
so much pain,
have my heart ripped
off my chest, again and again.

I had to rebuild
myself, coat every crack
throw the tears, before I drown,
behind my back.

I had to strip through
a lot of lies that dressed up
in shades of true.
But perhaps it was all worth it
because in the end...

I found me
in you.

603.

He tucked
my hair
behind my ears
snatched
the sadness
out of my tears
and said,
"let's break up
with all
of our fears".

And we took that leap.

***

In Arabic
we don't say "I'd die for you"
instead we say "I'd die in you".

That is why
when I fell
in love with you
I was no longer afraid
of falling…
For if I fall, I'd fall in *you.*
For if I die, I'd die in *you.*

604.

I say
'I
love
you'

And it
feels
like a
sacred
prayer.

I say
'I
love
you'

And it
looks
like a
temple
I
built
with the foundation
being
you.

'*I*
love
you'

605.

When we make love
my small body feels
like a grand temple
as his large body
crouches onto his knees
in worship.

My pleasure
his discipleship.

He makes love to me
like a religion,
in which he will never
sin.

My pleasure
his heaven.

He's memorized
the way
to the melody
of my orgasm,
like a prayer
rolling on his tongue.

His heart drums
onto mine like an ancient
song
of which our bodies belong.

And we dance…

Into climax
of this never-ending
romance.

***

My legs wrap
around his waist-
like a burrito
holding on
to delicious filling
in haste.

606.

A treasure chest;
An armour vest;
A place to rest;
His chest.

***

Perhaps I want to be an object.

An object of desire
of the subject I chose
to ignite my fire.

***

For so many years
I was so conflicted;
how can I be a feminist,
yet enjoy sexual submission?

Until I understood
that what I desire is to submit
for pleasure-
not for oppression.

N.B. Perhaps it is internalized misogyny that discourages women from exploring non-vanilla forms of sex because we shouldn't be exploring sex at all?

607.

I will try to capture
those years between
how it began
and
how it ended.

That part of the story
after
the foreplay,
and before
the orgasm.

608.

He plays
my clitoris like a clarinet
as I moan in melody.

Perhaps for a century.

And I know
this is what's been distracting women
from overthrowing the patriarchy.

We too often pause...
to make love
with the enemy.

***

This war we're fighting
silently,
sleeping
with the enemy.

It is chilling
that in those same beds, as our love sheds,
we give life
to misogyny.

609.

Flowers grow in the sand
as we walk hand in hand,
treading on sheets of brown
our toes, bowing down
to borders of endless blue.

The sea doesn't separate from the sky
blurred lines, where walls used to be.
My people have killed yours.
Your people have killed mine.
Maybe it's time… to love you… to love me.

***

In a past lifetime
he was *Romeo* and I was *Juliet*
he was the moon and I was the sunset,
distanced
destined
to be apart.

In this lifetime
he is *Sunni* and I am *Shiite*,
but the hate they taught us
has been killed
by the love in our hearts.

610.

They said
we cannot be buried
in the same cemetery.

The Sunni are buried in the East.
The Shiite are buried in the West.

We fought battles to live together.

But in the end
in death,
they will do us part.

***

And as I wait for you,
my darling-
the world stops
spinning,
and the deserts learn
how to weep.
Even time
goes fast
asleep.

611.

He wants to keep things the way they are
but I want to know for how long and how far.

He wants to take my today
but I want to take his tomorrow.

It's tense.

Because we are not living
in the same tense.

612.

My boyfriend…
are the two words
I can never,
dare to
utter,
because if I say them
in a culture where
I'm not allowed to make love
to anyone there,
except a husband,
saying that I have a *boyfriend*
is saying that
I broke the rules, broke the doors
of a hymen
that is no longer intact,
broken like a broken pact.
So I have to put on this virginal act
pretend I never dated
pretend that I waited
for a husband
and even then
for him to believe
I'm not guilty under my sleeve
I pretend he's my Adam
(while I know I'm not his Eve).
I pretend I don't know about sex
how to feel pleasure, how to love,
how to orgasm
by rising to heaven,
with just enough
lust to burn in hellfire-

I pretend and pretend
until I actually begin believe
that I never had a boyfriend
and that I don't have any sexual desire.

***

Those bed sheets I lie under
each night,
have seen bad dreams, bad boyfriends, bad breakups.
Yet they're still soft.
Nothing has hardened them-
even though
they've been through a lot.

613.

I have learned
how to
grow
thick skin
like the dense
brown soils
that cover the earth.
I am safe
holding onto my girth.
But every now and then
I crack again
and the rains pour in.
They get to me
in me
and it hurts
and it makes me recoil-
but then just as quickly
soft flowers start to grow
out of the dense soil.

                              ***

After drinking a drizzle of cries,
from the skies,
flowers begin to rise.

There's a lesson here, to realize.

When the clouds

slowly drift, away
like the shadows of lovers
who leave, without explanation-
the rain provides clarification.

Let it flow.

It's okay to cry,
when you don't know
why.

Your tears are not weakness-
you need to shed them, to shred ex-lovers with them,
to unravel yourself
then plant yourself,
above.

Sometimes you need dirt, and soil, and fuckboy turmoil,
to see that the only way you'll rise, like a flower
is through self-love.

***

You think you're letting go,
but you're actually holding on
only to what matters.

614.

Giving you
a second chance
doesn't mean I have
forgiven
you.

It simply means
I believe there is
more good than bad
in
you.

615.

Your eyes
ask me
why I stopped
putting on makeup and shaving my legs
for you.

Your eyes
accuse me
of being lazy
and perhaps, ugly too.

Your eyes
wonder
if this is the end
of our relationship too.

But fuckboy, it's clear;
you've never had a woman feel
that comfortable around you.

This was me, thinking you're worthy,
I was ready
to unravel my natural
beauty from *beauty myths*
to you.

616.

"You're mansplaining, ghosting,
gaslighting, sealioning..."
I told him.

"What the fuck does all this mean?"
he began to shout,
"some people just made up some names and you're just throwing
them out
at me?"

"No" I replied with glee,
"some people didn't just make up some names. You make it sound
like a myth-
some people finally gave a name
to the toxic behaviour
you've been getting away with".

617.

To the
woman married
to the
man I loved-
I'm sorry.

He told me you were separated to be divorced,
he cried until his voice went hoarse,
and then he spoke about you with so much hate,
I didn't realize, he was making me participate
in causing you pain.

He didn't want to take all the blame.

Yes it's his responsibility, yes he's the one who committed adultery,
but I was his partner in crime.

He said it was your fault, for not being sexually playful-
but he was playing us both,
at the same time.

I should have known. Dogs love hunting for bone.
Of course, he wouldn't leave you and the kids-
you're the main course, I'm the side dish,
he wants us both.

Oh how I wish,
I realized all this
sooner.

To the

woman married
to the
man I loved-
I'm sorry.
I didn't realize what I'd done
until I became,
a married woman.

N.B. It is not your fault.

***

To the
woman who loved
the
man I married-
I'm sorry.

He told me you were a stalker, who wanted us to get divorced
he said you were threatening him with force,
but he was actually taking you out on a date,
I didn't realize, he was making me participate
in causing you pain.

He didn't want to take all the blame.

Yes it's his responsibility, yes he's the one who used your
vulnerability,
but I was his partner in crime.

I saw the strand of your hair and your lipstick stain, he told me it was
just one time-
but I didn't warn you, that I knew,
he was playing us both,
at the same time.

I should have known. Dogs love hunting for bone.
Of course, it's not just a fling or a flirt-
I'm the main course, but you're the dessert,
he wants us both.

Oh how I wish,
I realized all this
sooner.

To the
woman who loved
the
man I married-
I'm sorry.
I didn't realize what I'd done
until I became,
the other woman.

N.B. It is not your fault.

618.

God is calling.
The dawn woke up in obedience.
The flowers rose from their graves.
The birds chirped in a choir of prayers.
I rinsed the sin
off my skin
to begin
to sing-
when my phone gets startled
from its own ring.

He is calling.
The man who never sleeps,
to make sure I only sleep
with him.
To make sure that he is the only
sin
to sink
into my skin.
He won't cleanse-
from this insecure jealousy
that he calls 'romance'.

He wants the loyalty of the dawn to the flowers to the birds to God to
me to him.

***

I said "Oh God! Oh God! Oh God!"
as we fucked last night.

And as the moon
began to spoon
with the morning light-
he believed he was God
with all his glory might.

***

She says "Oh God!"
He says "I'm coming- oh yes!"

And that sums it all.

She sees him as God.
He sees her as an object for sex.

619.

WARNING:
Men who don't like
reading maps
or following instructions as is-
will never ever
find
your clitoris.

620.

He imagines her
he forces her
the way he wants her
always young
always groomed
skilful tongue
a vagina perfumed-
an object
a product,
to be consumed.

He clicks on her picture
a holy scripture
so many of her,
to depicture.
From one to the other
he doesn't care,
they're all the same
doesn't bother, to know their name
all he wants, is to re-imagine
the rough fuck of an old flame.

Then he plays her video
imagines it's just for him
she spreads her legs
starts to beg
horny as fuck
plays with a dildo
anywhere it will go
any kink he enjoys
with another girl

with two boys.

"Harder, faster"
"Take me deeper"
that's exactly what he wants to hear,
she's a keeper.

And then he's done
had his fun
enjoyed her 'cooter'
enough of her 'hooters'
clears his history
shuts down the computer.

And just like that
she's quietly gone
out of his life
until the next time
he wants some fun
then she becomes
his someone
or maybe he replaces her with
another one
there's no preferred one
or a loved one
it's not long-run.

Her sad story will begin
again and again
after his many happy endings.
And what is so contradictory
is that he is the cause of her misery.
Here's the part

that breaks the heart
he does his best
to tear her apart.

"Whore! Tart!"
"She thinks she's smart?"
"Good for nothing, but legs apart!"
"Wants to be free? But she belongs to me-
to fuck and violate, that body!"

"Slut! Bitch!"
"Burn the witch!"
"Pretty woman- uses men, to make her rich!"

Until the night time comes
and he wants to come
suddenly, again
turns his computer on
"She's treasure…"
"A pleasure…"
"Leisure…"
"Happiness…with no measure"

He's a user
abuser
a fucking loser
he knows that if she's in front of him in real life
he can't arouse her
or amuse her,
so he decides to accuse her.
She's just something to demean,
a moments' pleasure, that makes him unclean.

But she is a person.
Alive, yet forced to mourn.
Shamed, yet makes you moan.
That is the problem (not with porn),
but with the way men watch porn.

                              ***

We shame women
for making porn,
but we don't
shame men
for watching it.

621.

As a heterosexual man
you literally,
have no right to say that
when a man exposes his limbs
it's not as sexually
attractive as when a woman
does the same.

You are not attracted to men,
so don't fucking mansplain!

***

Women are sexualized
but not allowed
to be sexual.

622.
I've had it!

I want to find that wire
in the circuit of my brain
that tells me
my sexual desire is a shame
and *snap it!*

***

Why must I
shame the honey
that spills from
my thighs-
because you believe in
virginity myth
lies?

623.
We desire sex
because we desire
home.

Each cell
in and on and between
our bones-
is built from sex.

How can we shame
such an act
without being ashamed
of our existence?

The taboo is not sex.
The taboo is the way
we've been taught to think
about sex.

***

In a world
that teaches us
our pleasure
is a shame and a sin-
a revolution roars
each time
a woman orgasms.

N.B. Also, research asexuality.

624.

He asked me
in all honesty
how many
lovers
I've had
before him.

So I told him:
if history matters so much
I want to know, too,
not how many lovers
you have consensually touched-
I want to know
how many women
you harassed, assaulted, or raped
because I am not bothered
by how much of your beauty
you gave away
to lovers before me.
What I want to know is;
when and if
your beauty can reverse into a beast
and how ugly
is he?

***

What if
we worry about our sons
becoming rapists
the way
we worry about our daughters
getting raped?

625.

I don't need you to tell me
to not be afraid
around you,
to let my hair down
to feel comfortable too,
that you aren't one of them bad guys
that you will never hurt me, your sweet tongue speaks honey
and tastes no bitter lies,
while you do not realize
the irony in the way you insist "don't be afraid"
you're *forcing* me to feel safe.

You. Are. Forcing. Me. To. Feel. Safe.

It doesn't work that way, when you ramble and rave.

And you expect me to believe you
to send my guards off-duty
to expose to you my heart, and then you'd rape with it my beauty.
I've been with so many of your kind, who pretend to be kind, and
come sneaking from behind
to invade my territories.
I can beat *Scheherazade* and narrate to you
One Million and One Nights
of stories,
about men like you.

I don't need you to tell me
to not be afraid
around you.

I listen to my own body, the way it reacts around the way you behave,
it tells me whether I am safe.
Whether my heart is calm, or is pounding
like an alarm.
Whether my skin melts or my goose bumps sink,
my body tells me, what your mind thinks.

I don't need you to tell me
to not be afraid
around you.
Don't mansplain my instincts.

We both know
the way I feel is true-
if I am safe, then you won't need you to tell me
to not be afraid
around you.

626.

"You're just showing off-
saying all those men catcalled you
or harassed you,
you're just trying to show me
that so many men want you"
he said.

So I told him
"You dickhead,
you cannot comprehend
the difference between
catcalling and compliments,
you think harassment is flirtation-
because your brain fetishizes
my hurt and my frustration!"

***

"I don't get it"
he said,
"if a random woman hollers
a sexual comment at me,
I'd be flattered and even happy,
but if I do it to a woman
she's offended instead".

"Because you don't see women as a threat"
I told him,
"your gender hasn't been
historically and systematically

oppressed by women,
that's why there's no such thing
as reverse sexism.
If a random woman hollers at you,
you'd automatically think
you're the best-
but if a random man hollers at me
I'd automatically worry,
what would he do next?"

627.

"Why did you put yourself in that situation?"
they asked.

I looked at them gobsmacked.

"To suggest that *any woman*
makes a choice
to put herself in such a situation,
you're implying that she *planned* her own rape as if it's an occasion,
and then went looking for a rapist
to accept her invitation".

                         ***

"She was asking for it"

Asking for what?
For attention?
Flirtation?
Admiration?
Perhaps the possibility of
consensual sex?

No one ever asks
to be raped by someone else.

628.

Asking for consent ruins the mood
only if you were in the mood
to rape.

***

Consent
isn't just about being comfortable
to say 'yes'.
It's also about being unafraid
to say 'no'.

629.

If I consent to go on a *date*
it doesn't mean I've consented to *hold hands*.

If I consent to *hold hands*
it doesn't mean I've consented to *kiss*.

If I consent to *kiss*
it doesn't mean I've consented to *undress*.

If I consent to *undress*
it doesn't mean I've consented to be *touched*.

If I consent to be *touched*
it doesn't mean I've consented to *oral sex*.

If I consent to *oral sex*
it doesn't mean I've consented to *penetrative sex*.

If I consent to *penetrative sex*
it doesn't mean I've consented to play your *sexual fantasy*.

If I consent to play your *sexual fantasy*
it doesn't mean I've consented to *everything else*
you'd like to do with me.

Consent is required
at *each stage*, and *each time*.

And just because I've consented *once*
it doesn't mean
my body is no longer mine.

630.

The biggest lie
men have convinced us
to believe
so that they can use
to justify and achieve
their sex crimes-
is that they are helpless
over their sexual desires,
and their sexual lust
is controlled
by a woman's body…
a body that is sexy but not sexual
because our sexual lust
is owned by a man's body.

Men blame me
for their sexual crimes.
And I blame men
for robbing what's mine.

631.

My mother taught me
to watch out for potential rapists
on the streets, in bars
at school, in church
on street corners, dark alleyways
so many locations
stored in the GPS
of my head.

But she didn't teach me
to watch out for potential rapists
I've trusted into
my own bed.

***

He is the most generous man
you'll ever meet
humble, down-to-earth, romantically sweet.
He is soothing balm,
as if words only exit his lips
to make the world calm.
He is raindrops on soft petals
and the skies of a thousand heavens
keeping bay at sea.
And he is also, too,
the man who ever so gently
raped me.

***

He plays so many roles.

Father, husband,
teacher, church-goer,
rapist.

He's the best dad and greatest husband
the most inspiring role model
and faithfully devout.

But he is a rapist too,
without a shadow
of a doubt.

632.

Can you stop for a second
to think about this:

Why is
believing a woman who says she was raped
(but turns out to be a liar)
is seen as so much worse than
believing a man who says he is innocent
(but turns out to be a rapist)?

Is it because the first one is about
destroying the life of an innocent man?
And the second one is about
destroying the life of an innocent woman?

633.

The way society reacts to rape:

Woman: I got raped.
Society: Are you sure?

Man: I didn't rape.
Society: We believe you.

The way society *should* react to rape:

Woman: I got raped.
Society: We believe you.

Man: I didn't rape.
Society: Are you sure?

***

He's innocent until proven guilty.
She's guilty until proven innocent.

634.

Let's normalize
believing women
without courtrooms
of evidence.
Because ever since
Adam blamed Eve
we've been believing men,
without any precedent.

N.B. In 2015, Pope Francis declared it was wrong that Adam blamed
Eve for his sin. (Source: www.corriere.it translated by Quartz).

635.

What a relief.

For me to tell you,
for you to believe.

                              ***

"I hope you know you're not alone"
my sisters told me
after I told them
about the rape.

They were trying
to comfort me
but I wept...
for the normalization
of our horrific fate.

636.

I believe.

Victims and survivors.

I believe
victims and survivors
because do you know
what they go through,
before they find the courage to
finally speak out to you?

-The actual horrific incident
-Processing the trauma
-Trying to justify, find excuses why, while staying silent because they
know they'll be accused of causing drama
-And victim blamed
-And shamed
-And perhaps be seen as weak.

I believe
victims and survivors
because they couldn't heal in other ways
when they finally found courage to speak.

637.

The part of your learning
that has reinforced victim blaming
is the one that makes you constantly
ask yourself
when reflecting on your abuse:
how could I have done better?

It is never your fault to begin with,
so how can you be responsible
for doing better?

***

Speaking out
against abuse
doesn't look the same for everyone.

There is no guidebook
no path, no trail,
you carve your own road
you're the pilot of this journey;
the pace is set by you.

The only thing I want to tell you:

Speaking out
against our abuse
isn't easy
because we have been ingrained

to stay silent about these matters.

We feel ashamed-
when it's our abusers
that should be shamed.

So if you decide to speak
no matter how slow or how fast
or what you are or aren't able to let out
about this heinous crime-
know that you are not only speaking
but also unlearning silence at the same time.

638.

Sometimes I remember.
Sometimes I don't.

Like the waves
in the way
the ocean flows;
it comes crashing all at once
and then it all goes.

***

Under my skin
my bones are broken,
but no one can see
the amount of pain,
my heart can carry.

Oceans.
Drowning emotions.

Sometimes
it's hard to speak
because I'm holding the tears
in my mouth.

My eyes have soaked so much
they have become drought.
When I speak, the entire ocean
cries out.

I struggle to find pleasure in sex
even while I'm masturbating
all by myself.

I touch myself
so tenderly,
yet my body can't trust anyone
even when
that person
is me.

Surviving rape doesn't mean you recognize the hands
that caused you pain-
all hands pull the trigger
even when
intentions aren't the same.

How can I set myself free,
from a rape that is no longer happening
yet still holding me captive
in its memory?

639.

I was raped by a woman.

It was during my early teens
I was curious about wearing a tampon,
she asked if I'd like help
putting one on.

I said "yes".
She pushed it in.
I pulled back, as the pain pierced my skin.
But she restrained my legs.

I screamed "STOP! YOU'RE HURTING ME!"
She got irate and angry
"Just a *second*! I'm almost done!"
That *second*
resulted in *decades*
of pain
that still live on.

At the time I didn't realize I was raped-
because there was nothing sexual about the incident
and initially I had said 'yes'.

But now I know
that consent is ongoing
and rape is not sex.

640.

I'm going to repeat this
until you don't believe anything else:

Rape is not "non-consensual" sex.
Rape is not sex.
Rape is not sex.
Rape is not sex.
Rape is not sex.
Rape is not sex.
Rape is not sex.
Rape is not sex.
Rape is not sex.
Rape is not sex.
Rape is not sex.
Rape is not sex.
Rape is not sex.
Rape is not sex.
Rape is not sex.
Rape is not sex.
Rape is not sex.
Rape is not sex.
Rape is not sex.
Rape is not sex.
Rape is not sex.
Rape is not sex.
Rape is not sex.
Rape is not sex.

N.B. Rape is not sex.

641.

He didn't hit me
but his words hit me
like a slap in the face.

He didn't force me down and rape me
but my lack of consent
was silently stripped
all over the place.

He didn't leave
any physical evidence
of his abuse.
I have no physical marks to show you
or any bruise.

He was smarter than to leave any trail-
there were no bars
but I was a prisoner
in his jail.

642.

"If you love me
don't make me angry..."
he constantly cried
as I constantly apologized.

It was only on hindsight,
when I started a new life, a new page-
I realized he was holding
me responsible
for *his* uncontrollable
rage.

***

He calls me "stupid"
because I won't take his bullshit.

He says "see-that's a nice conversation"
when I don't purge with disagreement.

He tells me to tell him "this feels good"
when I'm not in the mood
as he pumps me with sex.
And when he's done
he reminds me "I'm a simple man, I want nothing else".

Nothing else.

I'm full of everything, I can't be *nothing else.*

He's convinced me that he isn't asking for much-
just a woman ready to listen, ready to touch.

He says he wants *me*
yet he can't see
that he's stripped *my all*.

He doesn't realize that what he actually wants
is a blow-up sex doll.

643.

I can see my best friend,
being eaten up
by a monster,
that she calls 'husband'.

Like a doll,
he's changed the way she dressed
he decides when and how they have sex
he tells her it's all in her best interest.

She believes him.

I can see him,
eating up
all of her voice,
as she nibbles on
the leftovers of her choice.

"You look flattering" he will say
"when you submit to everything I say-
dressed in obedience
you look so good,
take off that ugly
feminist attitude".

He doesn't realize how badly he misunderstood,
love.
She tries to explain, but when he's challenged he screams again;
ENOUGH!

I can see my best friend,

being eaten up
by a monster,
that she calls 'husband'.

She has become skin and bones
with no soul.

She wants his heart
to love her,
but he wants her lungs
under his control.

644.

My mother told me that
"a woman can't get a new husband every day".

He insulted me
but I stayed
because "a woman can't get a new husband every day".

He cheated on me
but I stayed
because "a woman can't get a new husband every day".

He hit me
but I stayed
because "a woman can't get a new husband every day".

He raped me
but I stayed
because "a woman can't get a new husband every day".

He killed me
but I stayed
because "a woman can't get a new husband every day".

And now
I have no more days
left.

645.

Let's flip the conversation
ask questions
in the right direction;
let's ask why we groom women
to depend on men
and then blame them
when they struggle
to leave abusive men.

Let's ask why we never ask abusers why they abuse,
but we eagerly ask victims why they don't just choose
to *just leave*.

Let's ask why we question survivors
instead of believe.

There are so many questions
that are left unanswered
because we never asked them.

646.

We don't teach girls and women
to recognize the signs of abuse.
Because that sort of knowledge
will empower them to choose
to leave...

Leave situations and people oppressing them,
burn down the systems created by men.

They will begin to see
the signs of misogyny
in the sex appeals they're encouraged to wear
or the objectification in covering their body and hair.

They will realize
the lies
when men say they're just offering safety and protection
while they are actually controlling through oppression
expecting submission.

They will abandon religion
and the idea that they must
eventually inevitably
get married and have children.

If girls and women don't know the signs of abuse
they won't realize what's causing their pains.
How do you know you're in prison
when there are no locks and no chains?

We don't teach girls and women

to recognize the signs of abuse.
Because we want to set their paths
and we don't want them to choose.

647.

Do you know,
how much power you hold
when you seal the letters
N and O?

That is why
they never taught you
how to do it.
And even when
you learn
how to,
they quickly snatch your power
by pretending
they didn't hear you.

N O
seal it
say it
like a prayer
rolling on your tongue.

NO
is a right
that is never wrong.

648.

They take away birth control
and ban abortions
but if we say "no" to sex-
they'll grab us by the pussy
without any legal consequence.

Our rights
shouldn't be made an expense.

N.B. The U.S. Supreme court upheld a Trump administration
regulation that lets employers deny covering birth control for women
on the basis of religious or moral grounds.

649.

The patriarchy controls
the reproduction process
by *shaming* women;

-Shaming us for abortions
-Shaming us for miscarriages
-Shaming us for taking birth control
-Shaming us for being child-free
-Shaming us for choosing a career over family
-Shaming us for ticks of biological clocks

But we still have the power
to unlearn shame, and not give any fucks.

It is not a coincidence that men aren't shamed by any of these things-
the patriarchy gives man the freedom to decide
if, when, and how many
children he brings.

N.B. Men have biological clocks too. (Source: Phillips, Taylor, &
Bachmann (2019), "Maternal, infant and childhood risks associated
with advanced paternal age: The need for comprehensive counseling
for men", journal MATURITAS, Vol. 125, pp. 81-84).

650.

Perhaps the only
true democracy
is the land
of womb.

It decides when and how it bleeds.
It decides when and from whom to plant seeds.

The womb is an independent
democratic state
bordered by bones,
making humans out of
estrogens and testosterones.

My womb is a democracy
that I carry
between my bones.

My womb is an anarchy
from which every man
is born.

My womb is the only land left
that men are trying
to colonize and own.

And they will never succeed.

For when I merely unleash war
and proudly bleed,
they all run away from home.

***

How can you be disgusted
by the blood that comes
out of a vagina,
when your blood came
out of a vagina?

***

Our only value
to the patriarchy is
to make more babies
to make more men.
Perhaps that is why'
our menstruation
disgusts the patriarchy;
it is a massacre mourning
the potential life
of a potential man.

651.

It started when I was eleven,
and ever since then,
for one week, every month
my period took over my life.

I couldn't go swimming,
or wear white
or my favourite panties
or have sex
or touch myself.

My cramps immobilized me
perhaps psychologically,
but I would never ever
plan a party
or take a trip
or travel
or arrange any sort of experience
while I was bleeding.

I am not being delirious, it is that serious-
heck, I would at times call in sick to work,
match my leave days
with my biological clockwork.

Each month I'd circulate my plans
carefully, around my menstrual cycle
because while I bleed I choose to remain idle-
for that week
I am a massacre of bloodshed
clutching my uterus while lying in bed.

But I realized that all this
anxiety and fear
is because I was worried I would smear,
my clothes,
or cramp through
my experiences.

All this because I was worried about appearing to be a mess.

But from now on
I'll go on,
with my plans each month
preaching my blood and my cramps-
like a fucking Goddess.

652.

Three drops of blood
deep, round
hit the ground.
I hear them loud
(though they made no sound).

I push the hanger deeper.
It was hanging lifeless in my closet-
wearing the clothes
that he took my soul out of
on that sunny day
when everyone was on their way
to church,
dressed in pearls and silk
to look pretty for God
so that he won't see
how hideously ugly
they are under their flesh.

I push the hanger deeper.
It was hanging lifeless in my closet-
its shoulders
dressed in pearls and silk
to look pretty for God
so that he won't see
it was bent at the edges
from the way that sin
forcefully pinned me,
from the weight of the world
growing in me.

I push the hanger deeper.
The way he pushed himself deeper
on that sunny day,
I learned from him how to be cruel to
what has given me love.

I push the hanger deeper.
It is the pen to write my eulogy;
Three drops of blood.
One for my life.
One for yours.
One for..........................

***

Why is it
called *pro-life*
when it is completely
not *pro-life*
of a pregnant woman?

***

They say abortion is sinful
because you're ending
the potential life
God planted
in your belly.

I knew it.

I always knew it.

I knew that man believes
he is God.

653.

The boy cried "wolf!"
just for fun
and when the wolf came
it wasn't believed
by anyone.

So unbeknown to them
the wolf began
to eat the men
tearing their flesh
raw and fresh,
one by one
when he suddenly noticed a strange creature
(a woman)
with a defiant incense-
she had somehow escaped
the barbed wire fence.

He wanted to taste her
delicious skin,
but he was a coward-
he needed her to cross over
to him.
So he began to intimidate her
by calling her names:

Slut, bitch
nasty, witch
crazy, cunt
whore,
prude,

spinster,
fat,
ugly sister.

When all that didn't faze her
he cried
"MAN-HATER!"
she jumped over the fence, to fight for self-defence;
and that's when he ate her.

***

They accuse me
of being a
man-hater.
But to hate men
mustn't I hate
myself too?

For while
I am half egg-
I am half sperm
too.

654.

Misogyny
is so deeply embedded
in the construction
of manhood,
to the extent that
if you're a feminist
you're accused of
being a "man-hater".

***

Feminism only puts off
the men
who get turned on
by oppressing women.

655.

He calls feminists
"man-haters"
but what he means is
his ego is so fragile and insecure
it needs to constantly be reassured
by a woman's love,
and he can't stand to see that love
invested in a movement
that loves anyone other than him.

I can love you
and love my rights too.
And if you think I can't love both truly
then you are the one who can't love me.

If you're anti-feminist
then you're pro-misogyny.

656.

To the man
who sees feminism
as an enemy to fight;
what rights do *you* **lose**
when *I* **gain** my rights?

                              ***

You're worried that
when I gain my rights
I will oppress you
the way you do to me-
you don't believe I just want equality.

What you are afraid of
is not me.
You are afraid of
the projection of your own reality.

657.

To the men who are upset
that in the family courtroom
women are more likely to get
child custody.

Guess what?

The archaic gender roles
of woman being child-carer
and man being breadwinner
are upheld by patriarchy.

Help feminists
to dismantle the system
to achieve equality-
or else do not complain
about inequality.

Because guess what?

The injustice you feel
that has favoured your ex-wife,
is the way all women feel
about every aspect of our life!

658.

For the kids
for the marriage to go on
to maintain the social status
for the phobia of being single
or being divorced
which is scarier than being beaten and forced.

For money
for shelter
for food on the table
clothes on her body
a warm bed to sleep in
even if she gets raped in-
she's convinced,
that he is her ruler.
Starvation and homelessness are crueller,
on her bones.

For diamonds
a high powered seat
a position of authority
that almost competes
with other men-
playing pretend that she's better than them.

For being wired
to be dependent on men
to be incomplete otherwise,
to believe you are a part of his rib
you need him to be whole.....
and many many other fucked up lies.

This is how women uphold the system of patriarchy
often without being able to realize.

***

The men who hate women
not so coincidently
also hate feminism.

And the women who hate feminism
not so coincidently
also have internalized misogyny.

659.

Dear Man:
You are macho
in your vulnerability.
You are strong
in your softness.
Why do you work so hard
to get rid of your feminine?
You are half sperm, half egg-
you are half woman.

****

Misogyny presents itself as toxic masculinity too.
Reflect on the behaviours men aren't allowed to do.

Men can only attack not get attacked.
Men can only be strong not weak.
Men can only be rational not emotional.
Men can only be violent not gentle.

Have you ever wondered why?

It's because a man would rather die
than be accused of behaving "like a woman"
if he gets hurt and allows himself to cry.

Have you ever wondered why
male victims of violence aren't taken seriously?
It's because we can't fathom the attacker being attacked-
it is only women that are bashed intensively.

Misogyny is married to toxic masculinity.

The world shuns men who behave like women
because the world shuns women.

Do you shun women?

Dear Man:
Do you know how you can be free?
Instead of fucking women,
go fuck the patriarchy.

660.

Do men have a type?
Because I've seen all types of men
eye me up.

The thin ones, the fat ones
the religious ones, the liberal ones
all seem to give me
the same lustful glare.

Do men have a type?
Or do they all just like a vagina on legs, and a head, draped with a bed
of hair?

661.

They convince me
that *not all men*
are misogynistic pigs
who objectify my skin.

Then they tell me
to wear a hijab
in the presence of *all men*
who aren't
my kin.

Because it's strangers (not your kin) that would objectify you!
they justify.

But aren't my kin also strangers, to other women too?!
I cry.

Fuck this nonsensical logic you apply.

***

We are told
that it's "not all men",
and then *we are taught*
to be wary of "all men".

662.

The "NOT ALL MEN" myth: A short story

Me: Studies show that men rape.
Men: NOT ALL MEN! Stop spreading hate.

Me: Aha. Okay, cool. On another note I have a date
with this guy I met online.
Men: Be careful- he might cross the line.

Me: But you said not all men.
Men: Sure, but some of them.

Me: But he could be from the "not all men" category.
He seems nice.
Men: He could also be from the "some men" category
in disguise.

Me: So you're saying I must treat ALL MEN as potential rapists,
until they prove otherwise?
Men: …

The End.

663.

He says "not all men"
but what he really means is "not me".

It's just that his ego is so inflated
he thinks that "all men"
are
"he".

                              ***

If, by treating women well,
you mean that you treat your
mother/sister/wife/daughter
well
while you treat other women
like shit,
then you're not treating women well
and you're still a fucking misogynist.

If the women in your family
are the only women you treat properly,
then you aren't treating *any* women well
except when they're your property-
the ones you own are treated well
to protect what you claim,
while the ones you don't own
you see as fair game.

Until you treat ALL women well
regardless of your relationship to them-

don't come telling me you treat women well
as if you're better than other men.

664.

When you say that you respect
women,
because you'd expect
other men,
to treat your
mother/sister/wife/daughter
properly-
then you don't actually respect women,
you merely empathize with them,
when you view them as
property.

                              ***

He's taught
to protect
his sister
then his daughter
and his wife.

And he's confused
protecting
with
property
for all his life.

665.

The father
who grieves
the birth
of a daughter,
does so because
he finally realizes
the gravity
of the patriarchal system
he upholds and perpetuates.

666.

In the Arab journey of life
children belong
to their fathers-
they are carried by nameless women
and then they carry the names of men,
to preserve a male lineage.

No one questions
this pilgrimage.

But I am the daughter
of a man
who travelled through
the canal
of a woman.

I am the daughter
of a male lineage,
born out of
women.

***

I am a woman
made out of
women.

Carved out of
the ribs
of women.

I carry my father's name
but it's my mother's womb
that carried me.

I'm force-fed patriarchy
but I inhale feminism.

My maternal bloodline
is my religion.

I am a woman
made out of
women.

667.

Equality and fairness
are not the same.

You are half egg, half sperm-
but a man created you from pleasure
and a woman birthed you from pain.

***

"Women created humans"
I told him.

"But not without men!"
he exclaimed.

"Of course not-
I am not denying that"
I explained;
"But let us not equate
a moment of pleasure
which results in ejaculation,
with the 9-month
physical (and emotional) labour
involved in human creation".

668.

It's been 3 years
since I had my c-section
but it still feels like
a fresh massacre
is invading my womb,
it is now home
to tissue scars
forming like
a constellation of stars.

I can't see
but I can feel.

I know it is real.

I'm always in pain.

Doctors keep telling me
that there's nothing wrong
get some rest and check-in again.

My womb is a massacre
that no one is fighting,
only gaslighting.

My midriff is biting.

I ran out of ways to explain-
shouldn't doctors at least know
that after a c-section
the wounds of a womb

may never wane?

I know it is real.

I'm not insane.

N.B. Read article "20 ways c-section complications still affect mom years later" on www.moms.com

669.

Motherhood
has got me so exhausted-
I need to sleep
for a 100 years non-stop.
Let me put it this way;
if I was the *Sleeping Beauty*,
I'd dump the prince
for waking me up.

670.

Sometimes
when I'm at the sink
I realize that
I wash
more than just dishes-
I wash away
hopes, and dreams, and
the wishes
of every woman
I ever wanted
to be-
but instead I'm here
in the kitchen
because my family
need me.

***

Sometimes
I feel the love
in my heart overflowing-
bubbling passionately
like a boiling kettle,
so I pour it in cups
and give some to
my father, my mother,
my siblings, my husband,
my son,
my friends, my colleagues,
and everyone

that I see.
And then I realize
there's none left
for me.

671.

Nobody hears,
the sound of a mother's heart
when it's falling apart
when it's failing to part
with a child, for a career...
with a career, for a child...

It's hard to choose,
when I've got everything to lose-
this is the promotion I worked hard for,
this is the baby I would die for
I have to pick one
there's no two, three, or four...

The choices are simple
the decision is impossible.
There is a myth,
that women can 'have it all'
tell me how?
because I'm starting to fall...

I go to work every day,
drop my baby at nursery-
he cries, I walk away
I leave my soul, in the hands of strangers,
I can't focus at work.
Is my baby safe? Is he in danger?

I finish work, I pick up my child
happy to reunite
after hours that feel like years

I'm here baby, now no more tears.

We go out, we go home
we sing, we play, we eat
we have the world
at the tips of our feet.

A few hours later, baby still wants to play
I am exhausted from a very long day
I still have to clean and cook,
baby wants me to read his favourite book.

The alarm rings in the morning, I am tired
if I miss work again, I'll get fired.
The boss isn't pleased with my work
"being a mother is no excuse", he says
but what's his excuse for being a jerk?

When I finish my job at the office
I have another job at home
I am the employee, I am the mom.
There's no time for social life
there's no time for life,
to be me, to be a wife
to go for a walk, to have sex
coffee, whispers, and pecks.

How can I balance, two full time jobs?
How can women 'have it all'?
How can we rise every day, when all we feel is the fall?

I spent so many years...
Figuring out my fears,

tearing away my tears.
And I wonder
whether the way to do it is by
copying all those other
happy working mothers
balancing it all together
just to post a picture on Instagram.

We can do it all. We can have it all. We can. We can.

How come nobody can...
hear the sound of a mother's heart
when all her life is falling apart?

672.

I wanted to be
the perfect mom-
the one who bakes
cookies and shit,
who goes to school plays
and actually loves it.

I wanted to be
the perfect mom-
the one who never swears
always pleasant,
views motherhood as
a Holy present.

I wanted to be
the perfect mom-
who loves playing games
and arts and crafts,
and when her kids make a mess
she just sweetly laughs.

I wanted to be
the perfect mom
so badly.

But here I am
so far from,
the perfect mom,
and not giving a damn-
because I've realized
that the perfect mom

is just the way
I am.

***

Once, I had a breakdown
when my baby
ripped my favourite shirt.

Then I remembered
he's ripped
my uterus
while coming out of me,
and suddenly
I wasn't bothered about my shirt.

You pick your battles
and you pick how it hurts.

673.

He began to say, to my dismay
"Women entered the workforce in 19..."

"Fuckboy", I interrupted,
"we were always in the workforce
cooking, cleaning,
raising kids, running chores;
entire nations, for entire humanity
built on our backbones.
This is work- we always worked,
our offices under the roofs of homes.
I don't give a fuck if you don't see this
as "real work" that deserves to get paid-
it is still labour that we learn and churn,
no one is born with the skills of a maid".

674.

"If my wife's boss at work
was treating her bad, being a jerk-
I would step in
and even get into a fight"
he said.

"That's not right"
I told him.

"Why?"
he looked baffled.

"Imagine if your boss at work
was treating you bad, being a jerk-
and then your wife steps in
or even gets into a fight…"

And before I ended
my hypothetical scenario
he said,
"yeah, you're right".

***

We don't need men to protect us-
We need men to be held accountable for the shit they do to us.
We don't need men to save us-
we need men to stop saving the patriarchy,

I don't need to be saved.
I need to be safe.

675.

"Go to school"
they said
because education
is what sets girls free-
not a prince or a fairy
tale land.

I went to school
because I wanted to understand
the world.

But at school
I was taught to never ever
question religion.
When I did,
I got detention.

We had a class called 'home economics'
where girls are taught how to cook, iron, sew, and other important
'skills of life'-
I didn't realize at the time I was being trained
on how to be a wife.

We had to wear skirts and the boys wore pants
not allowed to cross-dress at all.
Those structural divisions
then appeared in all aspects of life
as structural controls.

"Go to school"
they said

because education
is what sets girls free-
but how can that happen
when schools are built
upon the patriarchy?

***

Men put the rules
to allow them to rule;
the system was never designed
to free us.

676.

Patriarchy and the Seven Sons

Once upon a time
there was a system named *Patriarchy* and it has seven sons. Let me
tell you briefly, about each one:

Racism is the eldest, and he sees White people as superior. The darker
your skin tone, the more likely you're inferior. There is no hidden
logic to this ulterior.

Xenophobia closely follows the footsteps of his elder brother. The
plan is set out so that he won't have to think for himself- so why
should he bother?

Capitalism is the comrade of *Classism*, dividing people into classes.
A few positions reserved at the top; even though the world is for the
masses.

Ableism cannot imagine a world that isn't designed for him. He cannot
understand why access and availability of spaces; from entertainment
to work places- is not just for him.

Homophobia's sexual orientation is straight. Every day he would
loudly and proudly narrate. He pretends to be 'afraid' of queers, while
he actually harbours a denial of hate.

Misogyny despises women, female, and the feminine. He punishes
men if they dare to exhibit any femininity. He's also happily married
to *Toxic Masculinity*.

Sexism is best friends with the "*Not All Men*" brigade. And they're very very mad, that this story doesn't have 'evil daughters'; "not all sons" are bad! But *Sexism* reassures them that each and every one presented in this tale- exists because the *Patriarchy* has fucked a female!

THE END (is what you make of it).

677.

Did you know that
hunters-gatherers
were an egalitarian society?

That only with the advent of agriculture
came the invention of patriarchy?

This major shift in human history
caused a combination of higher morbidity
and higher fertility,
while women took on the burden of this responsibility,
men took ownership of all the property.

And so property was passed down to the male lineage through
inheritance-
thus upon marriage, women began re-locating to their husbands'
residence;
this created a "patrilocal" precedent.

Because they owned no property,
women themselves were passed on like property
valued only for sex and had restrictions on their sexuality
to ensure a man passed down his property to a true heir.

The patriarchy started and took off from there,
then it gave birth to further inequalities;
sexism
gender discrimination
the class system
capitalism
slavery

anti-Black racism,
embedded in our laws and social systems
amplified and justified
through religions-
those are the origins
of how our world
came to be fucked up today.

Remember that next time someone tells you patriarchy is in our nature
asserting it's because men are physically greater.
Because the only reason physical strength would be needed to
accomplish a patriarchal mission,
is if women had to be beaten into submission!

N.B. Read into the Neolithic Revolution.

678.

"Women are too emotional"
is a phrase we often hear
as an excuse
to exclude
women
from positions of power
in court and government
because women are not afraid to cry or feel the softness of their souls.
They say we cannot possibly bring empowerment.
But are women, really, too emotional?
Or are they, as human beings, 'normal'?

When men were boys
they were taught to avoid
feeling
crying
they were told "to be a man,
you must not express
gentleness-
the only feelings you may feel
are anger
and violence".
So they grow up groomed
out of their emotions
buried inside an iceberg, frozen.
And when they get upset
they cannot logically process,
instead they erupt like a volcanic explosion.

Women feel, with all the depths of their humanly density
men suppress their emotional capacity,

so relatively,
correctly-
should we say that "women are too emotional"?
Or that men are trained to be paranormal?

***

"Men are physically stronger than women!"
he roared.

"Women are strong too" I told him,
but he ignored
me
as he kept making it seem
like a competition
persisting on his position.
"But who is physically stronger?!"
he kept stretching it longer.

So I asked him
"Do you ever ponder,
about the strength it takes
to endure menstruation?
The unspoken pain
of ovulation?
Do you ever wonder,
about the strength it takes
to go through pregnancy and childbirth?
And the strength women have
to carry every single person
that walked on this earth?

Don't fucking tell me that kind of strength
has no worth.
Don't fucking tell me men are stronger physically
we are different biologically (obviously)
but we each have physical strengths
equally.
Don't compare the strength of your fist
with the strength that makes women persist,
it's like apples and oranges...
different fruits, both have benefits".

679.

I learned about inequality and misogyny,
by watching myself through the eyes of
our fathers, brothers,
uncles, and lovers.

I learned about complicity and silence
in this system of patriarchy,
by watching the behaviour of
our mothers,
and aunts, and grandmothers.

And I learned about fighting
for women's rights to be free,
by watching how much
the world was breaking me.

680.

His eyes sadly grow
as he shows me pictures
of London, 120 years ago.
"Look how women used to modestly
dress..."
he says
"Would you take a look at that?!
Why are they now, oh so
scantily clad?"

"Times have changed, Father"
I told him.

Do you know what those women
went through?
They thought it was their fault
when men rape
they layered themselves in all this drape
and it took years for them to see
no matter what they wore
their bodies were at war
and they cannot ever be sure
that they would be safe.
Have you read the stories that those women wrote?
How they fought
to get the basic human right to vote,
and how they got beaten, jailed, even killed
for simply wanting to speak-
those clothes are now a symbol of a time
where strong women were seen as weak.
Why do you want us to go back?

We are the women of this week.

Times have changed, Father.

The times that cling to these clothes
no woman wants to relive those,
days.
We are here today-
I can study, vote, own property, and have a say
and tweet to the world #MeToo
without the shame of being a victim of violence
because the women before me shed off those clothes, and with them
they stripped from their silence.

Our clothes today, resemble resilience.

Being modest or scantily clad
in itself, is not what is bad-
what is awful is what
"modesty" vs. "revealing"
embodies.
Times have changed, Father
but men haven't- they still see women
as merely bodies.

681.

Have you heard men
talk about their cars
as if talking about a woman?

"She's so sexy"
"Look at her wheels"
"That beauty is all mine".

Has it ever made you feel
a tiny bit uneasy
like a slow shudder down your spine?

Reflect.

If yes,
that's because they talk about women
the same way,
and now you're watching them do it to an object.

It feels uneasy because it's easier
to realize what "objectification of women"
actually means
while you're watching it happen
to another "object".

682.

"So, compliments are offensive now?"
he asked when I told him not to call me pretty
"so feminists think it's a bad thing to throw a compliment your way?"

I told him:
No. Compliments are not a bad thing.
In every place you look you'll see,
women are complimented
and celebrated
only for being pretty.
It's not a bad thing to be called *pretty*-
it's not bad at all,
but when that's the *only* thing you're called
then it's harmful....!
It's rooted in an oppressive ideology
of a society that teaches girls and women, that the only significant
thing they can ever aspire to be-
is pretty.

I am not a geometric shape,
a jigsaw piece designed to fit
what your eyes desire to see-
so yes, fuck the way you chose to compliment me
I've heard enough of that narrative,
get creative,
and finish your sentence,
when you call me 'pretty'.

Because I'm not just pretty.
I'm pretty fucking awesome.

683.

Is it too farfetched
to suggest
that makeup is designed
to keep us idle
to hold us down?

Tell me, have you ever eaten a burger while wearing lipstick
without looking like Bozo the clown?

Like corsets and heels
women fashions are just for sex appeals,
designed for us to be seen
without comfortably seeing.

Stripping the 'human' from our being.

***

I object to being
an object.

684.

In a world that forces me
to crouch into a certain size
that I must aspire to be,
the women who walk tall in their skin
whatever size they're in
are the ones who give me permission
to aspire to be me.

***

To the woman
dressed in self confidence;
you look amazing
dressed in you.
Perhaps you can teach those
fashion designers
a trendy thing or two.

***

Instead of striving
to gain weight or lose weight
to be a bit thicker or a bit thinner,
strive for not worrying about what you ate
for dinner.

By that I mean
strive to be happy-
let go of counting calories

eat healthy, and indulge in guilty pleasure.
Stop looking for validation
from your scale, and your mirror.

And tell me,
what is that weight
where your heart feels
the lightest?

685.

LB: At last! We finally meet!
VV: Yeah because you finally realized you should just retreat!

chuckles

LB: I've heard so much about you...
VV: Me too...
Together: From the men we both made love to!

chuckles

LB: I can't believe we've been in the same neighbourhood for some 30+ years but we never met...
VV: I can't believe you have a twin that you haven't told me about yet!
LB: Well, we're not identical...

chuckles

LB: Let me properly introduce myself, my name is *Left Breast*, I've been around North, from U.S. to Europe, now sagging to China--
VV: Welcome to the South! My name is *Vulva* but the world insists on calling me *Vagina*!

N.B. A conversation between my saggy *Left Breast* and my *Vulva*.

686.

Let's normalize;
stretch marks
cellulite
tummy rolls
back rolls
jiggly thighs
wrinkly eyes
white hair
hairy legs
saggy breasts.

Let's normalize
what's normal.

687.

"When women see a man
drenched in a sweaty workout top
they have sexual fantasies"
he told me.

"Really?"
I asked him
"Do you think that is what women fantasize about,
or is this your male fantasy about
what you would like women to
fantasize about?
Wrapped in your own ego
seeing yourself as an *Adonis*
wherever you go-
and even while you're in a drench,
you think women fantasize
about your body odour stench?"

***

The man of my dreams
should have a thick dick-
I don't care about
personality, aspirations, or sass.

Because why is it that
when a man describes
the woman of his dreams-
he only cares about
big boobs and ass?

688.

The world on TV is created by men:

-Young women are beautiful
-Older women trying to look young are beautiful
-A man's looks don't matter
-Older women who do not try to look young, are aging
-Older men who do not try to look young, are sexy
-Fat women are funny, never sexy
-Thin women are sexy, never funny
-Women never get periods or period stains
-Women are always in the mood for sex
-Saying 'no', means keep pushing till she says 'yes'

The world on TV is a man's fantasy
and a woman's painful reality.

***

Directors
defend their use
of violence against women
in the movies,
by claiming
that they are raising
awareness on reality.

If that's the reason
then why do we never see
the reality of

women with cellulite
or jiggly thighs
or hairy legs
or not in the mood for sex
or having an occasional
period stain?
It's almost as if
those directors have a fetish
of seeing women in pain.

They're not raising awareness on reality.
They're glorifying violence against women.

689.

To the woman,
who looks down on women
for not having:

the right hairstyle
the right body size
the right clothes
the right shoes.

To all those fashion advice shows:

Fuck you.

Fuck you.
For participating in patriarchal abuse.
Fuck you.
For taking away another woman's right to choose.

You think you know what's trendy? You think you know what's right
for me?

Can't you see?
You are wearing misogyny-
and it isn't flattering.

There is no right way, or a one way
for what a woman must look like on any day-
unless you think women are objects
existing, merely to be on display.

N.B. Why don't we have those fashion advice shows for men?

690.

Hate speech,
death threats,
and
misogynistic comments,
all bypass
social media algorithms-
but dare post a picture
of female nipples
and you're blocked off the system!

This logic
fucks my mind;
how can a woman's naked body be more offensive
than the profanity
of humankind?

691.

If I could walk outside
without fear...

I would look men in the eye
without worrying
that if I was intimidating
I could die.

If I could walk outside
without fear...

I would wear my favourite dress
without worrying
that my "no"
could imply "yes".

If I could walk outside
without fear...

I would walk alone at night
without feeling
that jolt of fright
each time I bump into my shadow
because it reminds me of that man I know
who stalked me years ago.

If I could walk outside
without fear...
the fog would finally
clear.

If I could walk outside
without fear...

***

Imagine if there were no men in the world,
not forever,
just for a day or two
what would you do?

Maybe you'll go out late for a midnight stroll
maybe you won't worry about rape or gun control
maybe you'll drink and dance and wear whatever the fuck you want
without control
maybe there won't be a female death toll,
from horrible men, thinking they're sent from heaven, to discipline
women
when they're really stalkers and trolls.

Maybe you won't feel like a glory hole
existing to be fucked by some asshole,
who has a fetish to cum in every hole.
Maybe there will be no birth control
sex will be fun, without repercussion
without falling in a loophole.

Maybe you won't care about your stomach rolls
enjoy an extra rice bowl.
Maybe you'll feel beautiful enough after all-
in your own skin, loving yourself from the outside in,
maybe you'll finally accept your faults and pitfalls.

Maybe your looks won't matter as much as your aims and goals.
Maybe you'll be confident enough to play all roles-
a career, a mother, and a lover,
with a fair payroll.
Maybe women can really have it all.

Maybe you can fill that hole in your soul
that misogyny stole,
to make yourself whole.
Maybe you'll easily get up, maybe you'll never fall.
Because you know you were born complete, before your defeat-
it's a man that reduced you to a piece of meat, after all.

692.

I'm against single-sex spaces.

I was attacked by a cis man
(who was stalking me for days),
in a public toilet with a clear sign that had a stick figure wearing
that cape from outer space.

Segregated spaces falsely imply
that inside I'm safe, outside I could fairly die.

Segregated spaces also send a message
that to be safe, women must stay isolated-
if they venture into a mixed space it's their fault; they should expect
to get slated.

Segregated spaces give a false sense of security
the goal should be creating spaces where we all co-exist safely.
Otherwise, if single-sex spaces are the way,
why stop at toilets? Why not segregate each place and each day?

This is reality.

The world isn't single-sex, and if we can't co-exist;
how safe are we?

693.

"But he's a good man, he goes to church"
they tell me.

I don't care whether he fears
God, enough to play a religious part.
I care whether he fears
breaking
a woman's heart.

694.

I never felt
close to God
inside temples
with walls that never shook,
or while listening to mullahs and monks
chanting prayers
from a thousand year old story books.

I never felt
close to God
from religion-
or the threat of hell
or the promise of heaven.

I only feel
close to God
in nature-
when I study the landscape of mountains and valleys and every
feature
in the face of the sky
every drop of the ocean, every sand grain that is
I.

I only feel
close to God
in an earth
with clouds that cry,
with people who make mistakes,
who laugh, who live
and who aren't afraid to die.

I only feel
close to God
when I'm with what God
created-
I never felt
close to God
with an image of God
that man fabricated.

***

I don't worship at temples.

I worship at oceans, and valleys,
and art galleries,
and that little tattoo studio.

I worship kindness; I have faith
in humanity, wherever I go.

I don't worship at temples
but I do have
a revelation-
I don't worship God, but I worship God
's creation.

***

There is a sense of calmness
that engulfs me
when I enter

a tattoo studio
a tattoo temple
an art temple.

I believe in art
I worship art.

The ink pierces my skin
like God's words on a priest's tongue.

I carry art on my limbs
like a nun's vows for a lifelong.

Art penetrates my skin
reminding me of the pain of hell,
and the beauty of heaven
and the patience we are created from-
for God didn't take a day to build Rome.

695.

When
the white azaleas are tucked
behind the ears of shrubs,
listening to the songs
of bumble bees-
I feel weak in the knees.

When
the soft blushing pinks of my soles
are kissing
the cocoons of coca brown soils,
tickling my toes in a foreplay tease-
I feel weak in the knees.

When
the coconuts that hang onto the palms
nestle like
the coconuts hanging between my arms
to find warmth in a spring breeze-
I feel weak in the knees.

When
my skin can taste the milk of daises-
pouring into my every pore,
it's not enough, I still want more, please-
I feel weak in the knees.

I feel weak in the knees because
I want to become,
one,
with the mists that flirt with the rain-

for I was made from this
then dressed in bone and skin
and shame.

I want to strip from my layers-
feel the wind, pass through the artery of my vein.
I want to sing, love, laugh,
and I want to be earth,
again.

***

If you're *looking*
for happiness,
you won't find it.

Happiness isn't something you look for.
Happiness is something you feel.

If you're *looking*
for God,
you won't find him.

God isn't something you look for.
God is something you feel.

696.

There are millions of Gods
but I choose to worship
love.

There are thousands of religions
but I choose to practice
love.

There are hundreds of countries
but I choose to belong to
love.

For what else are we
made of?

My race is human.
My language is hope.
My country is love.

My dream is for...
all of the above.

***

When you realize
that you bleed
and wolves bleed

and birds bleed
and bees bleed
and fish bleed
and trees bleed…

You will realize
our pain is one.

697.

What is happening
in the mind of a human
playing God;
judging
deciding
who deserves rights
and who doesn't?

The world was made big enough
and we are all made from love.

We all deserve love.

***

God is just
the adult version
of Santa Claus,
and we're willing
to hate, fight, and kill one another
over his presents.

***

If all this hate, killing, and massacres
are done for
the love of God...
what can

our hate of Satan
do?

698.

According to the teaching of Talmud
you learn the Torah in the womb
and then at birth you forget it.

According to the teaching of Fitra,
you are born as a Muslim
by instinct.

Perhaps in the birth canal-
after you forget the Torah
and *before* you become a Muslim,
is the neutral land
where you understand
peace.

***

Religion is built
on the premise
of 'divide and conquer'-
for us to love God
we must hate one another.
For if we truly loved one another,
we would hate God.

***

I don’t hate Jews,
I hate violence.

I don’t hate Muslims,
I hate violence.

It is about time we see,
the real enemy.

Violence loves to play dress up
and for centuries,
it has dressed as
you and me.

699.

I don't understand why
I have to pick one religion;
one favourite book.

My mind can house libraries.
My heart beats through all
storytellers' hooks.

***

What if
we're all
Gods?

What if
I'm right
and you're right
and they're right,
and we create a world
where we peacefully unite?

700.

Religion saves me.

When I'm in a place
where people are living
in a time of centuries ago
yet I'm living in the today
and I don't believe their beliefs apply
to this time and day-
I pretend to believe in their way
anyway
recite some religious verses I know
because otherwise to jail I'll go...

Religion saves me.

When I want to go out on a date with a new lover
and I know if people saw me
they will report me to my father,
or to police authorities
because premarital dating is sinful and morally wrong-
I wear a niqab to hide my face before I go along.
No one would question
an invisible woman...

Religion saves me.

Whenever I don't feel safe
in my own home, in my own skin,
when religious people
terrorize and threaten-
religion saves me.

Religion saves me
not by inducing in me piety.

Religion saves me
(by hiding me)
from a religious society.

***

It's not harmful
to value religion-
what's harmful is when
you value religion
over your fellow human.

701.

I have a right to express
the oppression of my religion,
as you do the enlightenment
of yours.

We could both be *Muslims*-
one feels free
the other feels forced.

There is no right way
to repent or remorse.

Text is malleable, flexible
and subject to interpretation-
you could see a heaven
where I see
eternal damnation.

***

They make up sins
from the tongue of God
to control my skin
and my life
and they see nothing odd-
that they fear my freedom
instead of fearing their forgery of God.

***

My body
is not political property.
My sexual orientation
is not determined by religion.

I'd rather live this life
happy,
than aspire to your
imaginary heaven.

702.

They taught me
to cover my hair
while praying
to God.

But God has created
every hair follicle
on my head and my skin.
So what is the point
of hiding it all
from him?

***

There are so many women
who are forced
to wear the hijab-
and when I say that
I get attacked
as if I said something
so absurdly sinister.

Because there are so many women
who have the privilege of choosing
to wear hijab-
so privileged, in fact,
they have the power to erase
the voice of their oppressed sister.

***

And I will continue speaking.

For I have the voice my mother never had.

And I will continue speaking.

Against the "bad Muslims", and the "good Muslims" who only care about their religion to not be seen as bad.

They fight over a book,
who's got the right hook,
ignoring that the ending is sad.

And I will continue speaking.

Women will not end as characters playing the role of an image our oppressor had.

And I will continue speaking.

Not for me.
For I am already free.
I have ripped my shackles with my teeth
and I'm swimming in a pool of my blood
looking for a key.
Not for me.
For the woman after me.
So she can have her key instead of her blood
to set herself free.

703.

"Your writing implies
that you think modesty is oppression"
she said, with suspicion.

"I don't", I told her.
"I think *forced* modesty is oppression,
which is what is prevalent
in Muslim
nations;
whether explicitly or implicitly
directly or indirectly,
whether government laws force women to veil
or societal frowns slut-shame women who reveal
their bodies".

She thought for a while
then said
"France bans the burqa, what does that make you say?!"

I said "The mini-skirt is banned in K.S.A."

She said "But the burqa is religious attire, the mini-skirt isn't!"

I asked her "What do you define as religion?"

She said "A belief system, from a source Divine"

So I said "What if my belief system tells me that it's fine
to wear a mini dress?"

She said "That's absolute nonsense!"

"Does any of this make any sense?"
I asked her,
"Look at us! The patriarchy has pitied us against one another
arguing who is worse and who is best,
while clearly
we are both oppressed!
For equality, the question we must ask should be;
why aren't any governments controlling
the way men dress?!"

***

I'm accused of being Islamophobic
for criticizing Muslim nations
that set laws for women to wear hijab.
But I will also critique any country
that *forces* women to wear
mini-skirts or any revealing garb.

704.

They accuse me
of Islamophobia
when I say I'm hungry
because religion and society
have swallowed my rights.

They gaslight.

They
threaten me
terrorize me;
make my living
a fright.

Perhaps I do suffer from
Islamophobia.

Perhaps they are right.

I have a phobia that Islam
would violently suffocate
my voice into the silence
of the night.

705.

I was born in a Muslim community
and I'm sick of other Muslims telling me how to behave,
when I refuse to be an obedient slave,
they tell me
I'm not being Muslim enough
or Arab enough,
whenever I try to question or tell them to fuck off.
Accusing me of acting 'White'
as if the desire for freedom is a birthright
for White people only.

They call me a rebel, so I guess that's what I'll be.

I am not contempt with this Brown fate;
not allowed to date
to choose a husband, or to make love to other women
or get a pixie haircut
or let my hijab rot
in the back of my cupboard.
I must swallow their rules
and not be all bothered,
breathe in while I'm being smothered
Or else I'm accused of being 'White',
how is that fair or right?

"You're not Muslim enough!"
they say.
As if Islam
is just a balm
that I'm not rubbing

on my skin,
as if it's a dress
that I'm struggling
to fit in,
as if religion
is just a certain *style*
to wear for forever, or for a while.

"You're not Arab enough!"
they say.
As if ethnicity
lives on my tongue,
or in the melody
of my favourite *Bossa Nova* song,
as if one can choose
their ethnicity,
as if it wasn't already decided
by the Arab blood in me,
from generations long.

"You're not Brown enough!"
they say.
As if my light,
mocha skin
makes me almost White,
as if I need a certain qualification
to verify my discrimination,
as if I am not the right shade
to claim that I'm afraid.

I'm tired of proving myself, tired of playing their game.

Then again...

Perhaps I am not
Muslim enough...
Arab enough...
Brown enough...
you see-
those labels were given
by my parents to me.

Perhaps I am figuring out
who else, what else,
I can be.

706.

Ever since I was a kid I remember
each Christmas my grandmother
would put out a tree
my grandfather brings presents
to all my cousins and me.
In adulthood,
I still recreate this
wonderful memory.

Born in a Muslim family
this is how I was taught
to understand, accept, and see
the beauty of
diversity.

707.

I laugh
when the world says
ARABS ARE TERRORISTS.

My Arab friends joke about it
we've internalized it, normalized it
with laughter all along.

But when I travel abroad
I strip Arab
from my clothes and my tongue.

Yet when I starve on foreign land
I eat Arabic food
when I yearn for the language I understand
I listen to Arabic songs.

I consume Arab, without producing Arab
because *being* Arab *feels* wrong.

And when I go back home
it feels like I travelled back in time-
nothing's changed in my mother's face
but she doesn't recognize mine.

"What's this nonsense about
women's rights to choose?"
she asks me,
"your marriage will be arranged
to your cousin,
you can't make friends

with Jews.
Your father will kill you
if he sees those tattoos.
Only immoral women
go out
without
curfews.
What's this nonsense you've imported
from Western feminists?"

And now...

I weep
when the world says
ARABS ARE TERRORISTS.

708.

We've internalized
the White voice
that oppresses our communities,
and we've internalized
the idea that freedom belongs to the White.

This is how we remain complicit and silent
and foreigners to the notion of human rights.

709.

I'm an Arab woman
but I don't write
just for
Arab women.

I write
for all women
for all men,
for all worlds
for all time.

Because you'll understand
your own experiences better,
when you listen
to mine.

                              ***

My fight in the East
is relevant to my Western sisters
because our fight
is one.

And when we free
the most oppressed,
we free everyone.

710.

"What colour are you?"
they ask.
And the correct answer, I'm taught, is:
"It doesn't matter, we're all the same",
I've swallowed it like the national anthem
of a country that forces you to sing
at your pain.

And it's true.

It's true you should be given the *same opportunities*
no matter what colour you are,
but it's untrue that it *doesn't matter*
what colour you are-
because this sort of naivety
erases your understanding of history,
privilege, and what's happening in the world thus far.

"What colour are you?"
they ask.
Growing up, I've learned
that there are two human races;
you're either White or a 'Person of Colour'
you're either God's favourite or an 'other',
and I knew I wasn't White
but I didn't know just exactly quite
what 'other' colour I am.
For my entire life I was content,
being a 'person of colour' with no continent;
when Blacks struggled I felt pain
when Browns struggled I felt the same

when Yellows struggled I felt it again.
Because I wasn't White,
so I belonged to every non-White category
I did not understand the significance
of our different
history.

I was Vincent Chin, and George Floyd,
I was the Mexican children at the border
and all the Palestinian homes destroyed.
In Europe, my father is often confused
for being Hispanic,
my mother thought to be Black,
my brother would immediately panic
if someone says 'Salaam'
to greet him back.
You see 'race' has an evil stepsister called
'stereotype', and she's laden-
that is why as an Arab and a Muslim I am,
paying the bills of Saddam,
and Osama bin Laden.

So tonight,
I want you to sit with your skin
come up with a better answer
to the question,
because yes, we can all come together
and yes, we can all do better
than what our ancestors did
or had to go through-
but to do that, you must first truly answer
"What colour are you?"

711.

I have a secret, that I'm dying to tell you-
sometimes
people don't see my colour
and I don't see my colour, too.

I'm Brown,
I'm light.

I could be White
or as White
as I pretend to be.

I speak perfect English,
I've abandoned my ancestry.

I don't remember how I forgot
my history.

I wear jeans.

I say "God bless you" when I hear someone sneeze.
And "Jeez!"
when I'm annoyed.
And "Jesus Christ..."
when I feel a void.

I'm not a Christian.
I've been to Church.
I've never touched a Bible.
I'm a Muslim.
I've never been in a Mosque.

Buddha is my idol.

I'm confused.
Do I have to choose?
I have best friends
who are Jews.

Like flowers out of mud
I pick love out of taboos.

When I'm happy, I listen to the *Blues*.

My grandmother marks her skin with *henna*,
I mark mine with tattoos.

My grandfather walked in the desert
without any shoes.
His blanket was the sky.

I live in a 27 storey tower
and I draw the curtains because the sun
feels sour,
who the fuck am I?

Though I still like drinking *chai*
but with a strawberry tart.

I love art.

I had a boyfriend who broke my heart.
I've kissed him,
I knew that's a premarital sin-
it's a secret I've buried.

But I kept my vagina
for the man I married.

He gave it back to me.

He helped me unlearn and see-
that sex isn't something I give away,
sex is also for me.

He's one hell of a man-
if I tell you more about him,
you'll know who I am.

My parents are first cousins
in Arab culture, this type of marriage is common.
My Western friends find it odd.

I am revolted by the idea
of fucking someone
with whom I share blood.

I have a bucket list
for a different lifetime,
it's getting too late today.

I never had a chance to discover
whether I could be gay.

I'll have to change the world,
one day.

For my son.

He's only 3
but he looks so much like me,
already.

He's ready.

To start his own traditions
except they all look Western-
and soon stereotypes will teach him
that his Eastern is terrorism,
and he, too, will struggle
to wear his Arab identity
because the world thinks it's scary
like a Halloween disguise.

He prefers pasta over rice.

I know he doesn't quite yet realize,
but I still whisper
into the mirror of his eyes;

I have a secret, that I'm dying to tell you-
sometimes
people don't see my colour
and it kills me,
that I don't see my colour, too.

712.

Race exists,
and it's important
to acknowledge it;
not so that we can
build up more walls
made out of the different
pigments
of our skins-
but so that we can
understand and dismantle
the barbaric system
our ancestors built
which we *still* live in!!

713.

We are just different shades.

Here I am
trying to wash away
the bondage of my ancestry
from my tongue.

Carving a new language
for me to belong.

We are just different shades.

The darker you are
the darker your world-
you didn't do anything wrong.

But my tongue can taste
the cry of *enough*.

It's enough.

We do onto the world
what is done to us
only when we only know pain
and never tasted love.

I have tasted love.

714.

My skin tone isn't just
my hardbound bone cover.
My skin tone sings tunes,
the lullabies of my grandmother.
It smells of rosemary
and a recipe
inherited from generations.
Each cell memory
echoes painful centuries
of cruel occupation.

We are all seeds
of our ancestors'
privilege or lived discrimination.

This skin shade
wrapped around my body
and my face,
tells stories
that history can't erase.

So how dare you say
you don't see my race?

***

Seeing 'race' is not a problem.
Being 'racist' is the problem.
Seeing race is empowering.
Engaging in racism is damaging.

715.

"I don't see race/colour"
(no matter how well-intended)
is a statement that is gaslighting
and reeks of privilege.
There are people getting murdered
because of their race/colour-
do you not see that?

When you say
"I don't see colour"
to another,
you're also saying
"I don't see how you suffer-
I don't see what you lost
or what you had to fight to gain.
I don't see any of your pain".

It is not racist to see race.
It is racist to be a racist.

Our skins
are merely the hardbound covers
of our stories.

***

Do you ever wonder
what it's like to be
a Person of Colour,
in a world that says
it doesn't see colour?

716.

If you don't see my
race/class/sexuality/gender/disability-
then you don't see your privilege
which allows you to not see my
race/class/sexuality/gender/disability.

***

Your ability to say "I don't see race/class/sexuality/gender/disability"
(no matter how well-intentioned) is an example of your not
recognizing that you have privilege. Your privilege is what allows
you to make such statements in the first place. You haven't
experienced suffering severe enough to allow you to recognize that
the suffering of others due to racism, classism, sexism, ableism, and
other forms of discrimination does exist.

How can you do your part to dismantle the system of privilege that
oppresses others based on their race/class/sexuality/gender/disability
if you don't even see race/class/sexuality/gender/disability?

How can you do your part to dismantle the system of privilege that
benefits you at the expense of others if you don't even see your
privileges?

And for those saying why would anyone dismantle a system of
privilege that benefits them- I say; why does it have to be benefiting

184

at the expense of others? Why would people not contribute to a system that benefits us all? There's room for all of us. The world is big enough.

An ideal world is one where we don't see race/class/sexuality/gender/disability because no one is treated differently based on their race/class/sexuality/gender/disability.

We are not living in an ideal world.

717.

I was at the last stage of the assembly line in the human factory,
I had all my essential organs and bones
and then God asked me;
"What skin colour would you like to wear?
the selection of shades are all over there-
take your pick from the inventory,
each comes with a booklet
of its own history".

So I browsed through the colours
of oppressors and oppressed.
I read all the stories about
the North, South, East, and the West.

I struggled to pick, which one is the best.

Which colour to wear in this day and time?
Will I be judged by its ancestors' history
or the future that is mine?

So I went back naked to the Divine,
and I said,
"None of those shades appeal to me
in any fashion-
so I don't care, which of those skins I wear,
but give me a heart
of compassion".

718.

I swipe
scroll down
with every flick,
a trigger clicks
news of another
innocent Black death,
a virus that still wants
to take my breath.
What's next?
I hit refresh
pictures of children
without flesh
just bones on skin
a war, a famine,
is Yemen
on the same planet
we live in?
What's next?
Rape. Rape apologists.
Trans- exclusionists.
Breaking: children stories aren't real.
How do I feel?
Reading quotes of motivation
"Be yourself, follow your dreams
use your imagination"...
well except if you're a woman-
pay your life for a ticket to heaven.
Checking my inbox;
dick pics get deleted
death threats get blocks.
Take a break-

come back to another death.
I swipe, scroll down, tears run down.
How long has it been?
It is privilege that I only see all this
from behind a screen.

719.

You chew the chocolate off my skin
then you claim it isn't good for you-
too sweet, too sugary
too much calories.

Dangerous.
Promiscuous.
Frivolous.

You chew the chocolate off my skin
then you throw me away
a pile of white bones.

And I'm expected to re-build myself
by myself, on my own
while my sweet was sacrificed
to build your people
and plump your home.

                                        ***

I often realize
it is the poor
that rely on
their faith
of God
to get by.

Because the rich
are
God.

720.

It wasn't *Jack* that died.

It was the working class
in a capitalist community
at a time of an existential crisis
(just like now with Coronavirus).
It was the idea that romance
can intersect and abolish classes.
Jack wasn't just saving *Rose*-
she represents all of those
who survive from the sacrifices
of the working class masses.

It wasn't *Jack* that died.
It was the hopes that the poor
can merely share with the rich
a fucking boat ride.

721.

That 1,000 storey
glorious building,
is made from 1,000 stories
of sad endings.
Each brick has been laid
by the sweat,
of unjustly paid
human debt.
Workers who left behind
their children and wives.
Workers building a future
of which they won't survive.
Workers who climbed to the top
only to tragically lose their lives.
Do you realize?
That every rich person
we've seen in the world,
built their fortune
out of voices
we've never heard.

N.B. One out of every five worker deaths is construction related!
(Source: OSHA- Occupational Safety and Health Administration, part
of the United States Department of Labor).

722.

When I was 11
I went to Mecca
and saw an Asian boy my age screaming
because a shop owner was beating him with a stick for stealing
a prayer mat.

His father stood there by his bleeding son
helpless to end the abusive spat.

And I wondered about those
who steal millions, from millions
of poor people
and they get away with it
without a beating from anyone-
because they create and own the system
that beats poor people
so that only the rich can keep stealing
from everyone.

N.B. Hand amputation is practiced as a punishment for stealing in
several countries around the world including Saudi Arabia, Yemen,
United Arab Emirates, Iran, Sudan, and Islamic regions of Nigeria.

723.

The economy of the home
is built from the backbones,
of women.

And multi-million dollar corporations
are forever in debt
to the sweat,
of the working classes.

The tragedy is that they think they're doing us a favour-
but it is from our unpaid or unfairly paid labour
that oppressors have power over the masses.

***

I will not tell you
to quit your job
because you are
underpaid,
while I know
there is no alternative
if you strayed.

It is not fair
to expect the working class
to strike collectively,
to force the upper class
to behave ethically.

Yes, this revolution
must happen,
but there must be a solution
for it to happen in a way
without asking the poor
to further sacrifice their pay.

The revolution
must flush out the bullshit
coming out of the rich asses.

Spread out
the finances.

The revolution
shouldn't be paid by the hunger
of the working classes.

724.

She finally
stood up
for herself-
not tolerating toxic
relationships
that hurt her feelings.

And while each one of us,
is mourning what we had, what we lost, our life outdoors…
the earth is beautifully
healing.

***

The conundrum is
what's killing us
is healing earth.

N.B. According to the *Economic Times*, the air quality globally has improved this year due to Coronavirus lockdowns. And, according to *Our World in Data*, Coronavirus caused an estimated more than half a million deaths worldwide thus far.

725.

I miss going out.

I miss queuing for overpriced *Starbucks* coffee
without having to worry
that the barista might accidently give me
a Corona- Latté.

I miss getting a sandwich from *Subway*;
it tastes delicious, but let me tell you this
if I inhale it, it stinks,
but the good news is
I'd get a work leave for food poisoning.

I miss the mundane need to just bask.
I miss going out without gloves and a mask.
I miss seeing people's faces.
I miss getting lost in crowded places.
I miss not having to worry-
the only thing I don't miss
is life moving in a hurry.

726.

Amid life with Coronavirus;
people who refuse to wear
masks while out in public
because it doesn't feel good,
remind me of
people who refuse to wear
condoms during sex
because it doesn't feel good.

It's not about how you feel, you fucker
it's about potentially harming another!

***

"Now with the Coronavirus,
we're told to wear masks and gloves
for protection,
Muslim women have been doing that for centuries
yet the West call it 'oppression'.
They laugh at us, but we're light-years ahead!"
he said.

Impressed with his line of thought.

"Believe it or not",
I told him
"they're still laughing at you, and I'm laughing too,
because you just proved that

the 'oppression' is true.
What's worse is that you don't even realize
how completely misogynistic you sound-
you are literally saying that
a woman is *naturally a virus*
so she must be covered from head to ground!"

727.

Did you know?

There are women who aren't inconvenienced by wearing face masks
and gloves wherever they go,
because they've spent their entire lives forced to cover their faces and
bodies from head to toe.

Did you know?

There are women who aren't inconvenienced by the shutting down of
airports, schools, and workplaces,
because they've spent their entire lives forbidden from travel and
study and work and the right to life's basics.

There are women who aren't inconvenienced by social distancing,
because they've spent their entire lives not allowed to attend social
gatherings.

Did you know?

There are women who aren't inconvenienced by the shutting down of
malls, cinemas, bars, and cafes
because they've spent their entire lives restricted from those places
anyways.

There are women who aren't inconvenienced by governmental
curfews,
because they've spent their entire lives without getting to choose
what time they can go out or come back home.
There are women who have never felt their bodies in flight
to make love to the stars past midnight

or even just aimlessly roam.

Did you know?

There are women who aren't inconvenienced by lockdowns or
quarantines,
because they've spent their entire lives locked up; seeing without
being seen.

This Coronavirus lifestyle has forced
me to reflect
on my reinforced
privilege-
for as an Arab woman, if my (male) family members weren't enablers
of my freedom,
to be free, my only other choice would be,
to abandon my lineage.

728.

This quarantine
that feels so unfamiliar
is not so unfamiliar
to that bird you keep locked
in the cage, in your kitchen
to chirp tunes
you think sound pretty.
And it is not so unfamiliar
to that dolphin, locked in your local aquarium
just so you have a place to take your kids
when you're out in the city.

This quarantine
that feels so unfamiliar
is not so unfamiliar
to the domestic worker
who lives locked in your house-
to cook, clean, watch your kids
and is often assaulted by your spouse.

This quarantine
that feels so unfamiliar
is not so unfamiliar
to the woman locked up in jail
because she killed her husband
after he killed every cell in her body
that she tried to bail.

This quarantine
that feels so unfamiliar
is not so unfamiliar

to those who are locked into oppression and abuse.

Perhaps this quarantine
will give oppressors a chance to reflect-
on the rights they quarantine from others
to choose.

729.

If
within just a few months of education
we've learned a new way of living
normalized masks and social distancing,
imagine
what just a few months of education
on privilege and systemic oppression,
would do to combat
anti-Black racism.

***

There's nothing
more dangerous
than a White narrative
which got us convinced
that every other race
is dangerous.

***

We're taught
that we're all
the slaves of God,
yet historically and continually
we've been enslaved
by the White man...

Is the White man,
God?

730.

We are all born free-
after captivity
in the womb,
after the bondage
of our umbilical cord
is cut with a sword,
we scream
when our lungs take
the first gulp of air,
freedom feels foreign
to the follicles
of our hair,
we struggle
we only feel safe
when we nestle,
into the bosom
of the body
that held us in captivity.
And some of us grow
to never know-
we are all born free.

***

Our skins aren't
made to be tombs.
We are all born free
from red wombs.

N.B. JUNETEENTH.

731.

A massacre engulfs the horizon;
troops invade
pains evade
victory in a
foreign language of weapons.
Mass destruction of bleeding
wounds gaping
begging for the sweet mercy
of death.

A massacre engulfs the horizon of my body,
and God didn't stop it
because he didn't know,
that I have a right
to say NO.

N.B. The "father of modern gynaecology" James Marion Sims
developed his work by performing shocking experiments on Black
women whom he enslaved. While most of those women's names are
lost in history, based on Sims records we know three of those women
(not all of their last names). **Say their names: Anarcha Westcott,
Lucy, and Betsey**. (Recommended reading: "The 'Father of Modern
Gynaecology' performed shocking experiments on slaves" in
www.history.com).

732.

"I CAN'T BREATHE"
I tell God, as my Black turns blue,
but God is a White man too-
so he takes from my breath
to give my killer more strength,
to shovel my grave
with his knee
to bury my lungs in the gravel
for all to see,
that as a Black man
like my ancestors preceding-
I am guilty for the crime
of breathing.

N.B. JUSTICE FOR GEORGE FLOYD.

733.
If
ALL LIVES MATTER
why are we seeing
that Black lives
don't matter?

Why did it take
8 minutes and 46 seconds
for a White man to kill a Black man
and 96 hours
for him to get arrested?
Why are the other 3
non-Black criminals running free,
but lockdowns are imposed
because Black people protested?
Why are governments angry,
over the lootings
and burning of buildings
not the shootings,
and the brutal killings
of Black human beings?

If
ALL LIVES MATTER
and you believe that to be true-
then surely Black lives
would matter, too?

***

If you believe
ALL LIVES MATTER-
you should be enraged
at what's happening
to our Black sisters and brothers.

***

"All lives matter"
is gaslighting.

If "all lives matter"
there would be no
racism, xenophobia,
capitalism, classism,
ableism, homophobia,
misogyny, sexism...
and more!

But not "all lives matter",
that's for sure!

734.

Racial killing
happens because of
Racial physical violence
which happens because of
Racial marginalization
which happens because of
Racial discrimination
which happens because of
Racial bullying
which happens because of
Racial "harmless" jokes/comments
which happens because of
Racial prejudices inherited from ancestry
which happens because of
Hate of the 'other'.

N.B. Are you aware how you participate in racial genocides?

735.

WE'RE ALL RACISTS.

Racism wears different dresses.
There's full-length participation,
but there's also ignoring, ignorance,
and silence to its dictation.

WE'RE ALL RACISTS.

You know how I know this?
Because Derek Chauvin wouldn't have felt safe enough to murder a
Black man
while being filmed
by an audience in broad day-
and George Floyd would have still
been alive today.

736.

Dear White people,
Don't apologize
for what your people have done.

Apologize
for what you haven't done
to stop them.

It's been going on
far too long.

Being an ally
doesn't mean
telling Black people
that you aren't racist-
it's calling out non-Black people
for their racism.

737.

If you're NOT Black
and also NOT White
you're not out of blame
in this fight.
Anti-Black racism isn't just
a White person's problem-
you're also as guilty as them.

THIS IS A WAKE-UP CALL
TO ALL,
IN THE NON-BLACK COMMUNITY-
NOT JUST WHITE PEOPLE,
WE ALL HOLD ACCOUNTABILITY.

CHECK YOUR BIASES,
CONNECT THOSE DOTS,
THEN LOOK AT THE BIGGER PICTURE,
AND YOU'LL SEE-
YOU'VE CONTRIBUTED
TO THIS TRAGEDY.

LISTEN, LEARN, CONFRONT YOUR RACIST DEMONS
BECAUSE IGNORANCE
ISN'T BLISS-
IGNORANCE
ACTUALLY LITERALLY
KILLS!

738.
Dear fellow non-Black Arabs,

This is for you.
Here's how in the murder of George Floyd,
we're guilty too.

If you're a non-White person, it's so convenient to pin the murder of George Floyd on White supremacy and move on. Shrug your shoulders, say it's not my fault, or even fight White supremacy without realizing you are still self-serving (in other words- you are not fighting White supremacy because it's killing Black people, but because you recognize it hurts you too).

But let's examine some more details of this violent murder. The cop who was shielding Chauvin was not White (Asian). The store employee who called the cops was not White (Arab). And if you're saying that the store was merely following fraud procedure- the store owner has since issued a statement saying that they are aware of police brutality and in future will not call the cops with such incidents. My thought is; if you were already aware of police brutality, why have you not used your awareness before making that call? Why wait for say, a man to get murdered, for you to say you won't call the police with such incidents?

Unless we (non-Whites and non-Blacks) can see and understand how we also contribute to anti-Black racism, the problem will still simmer in our world.

***

As a Brown Arab woman, I am going to call out my fellow non-Black Arabs on our contribution to anti-Black racism. This is not a White person's problem only, we are guilty too. No matter how explicit or subtle, all those dots connected to lead to the tragic death of George Floyd. Below, I will recount to you JUST A FEW examples of insidious anti-Black racism that I see daily while living in an Arab country (I encourage you to reflect and think of more examples):

-When referring to Black people we use the words "aswad" (which means Black) and "abid" (which means slave) as synonyms.

-We have Black friends, but we aren't allowed to marry them. Interracial marriages are still taboo in Arab culture. I cannot even think of one interracial Arab couple in my radar. Not a celebrity. Not a friend. Not a random passerby. Not one. But I know many hearts broken because they couldn't marry a Black person they love.

-Have you seen Myriam Fares' blackface music video? Have you seen the countless Arabic movies and shows where blackface is just part of the comedy? What's your reaction to them? It must be silence or acceptance because it's 2020 and we still have that shit streaming on our TV screens!

-Open your phone's photo gallery right now. Tell me you don't have at least one meme sent by a friend where a Black person is the subject of the joke. Racism is NOT funny. Racism KILLS.

If you tell me those behaviours are not comparable to murder- I will tell you that such behaviour IS a part of a system designed to murder Black people. Do you want to endorse that system in your day to day?

***

Fellow non-Black Arabs; it might feel uncomfortable when I tell you that we are part of the problem. I have heard, spoken to, read comments on social media, from non-Black Arabs going on the defence mode when their racism is called out. But you know what's the RIGHT reaction to your discomfort instead of going on defence mode? You must be saying FUCK MY DISCOMFORT- BLACK PEOPLE ARE LITERALLY DYING AND HERE I AM FEELING OFFENDED BECAUSE I DON'T WANT TO REFLECT!

***

Fellow non-Black Arabs, here's what we can do now instead of going on defence mode:
-DONATE to Black fundraisers.
-READ to learn from Black authors.
-REFLECT on your own biases and unlearn them to dismantle the system of privilege you're born in.
-CALL OUT racism, no matter how minor. Don't be silent. Use your space to be a loud noisy ally.

***

Fellow non-Black Arabs; there's a deadly pandemic infecting our brains and killing Black communities. Our children are inheriting it. To combat it, you need to first be aware of it, acknowledge it, then unlearn it.

739.

I don't see burning or broken buildings-
I see burning lungs in Black bodies
who simply don't want their breathing
to be broken.

I don't see theft or lootings-
I see a few days attempts
to take back, what for centuries,
was already stolen.

And for all those judging me-
I don't see how you can't see,
that the immoral cannot understand
the language of morality.

***

Repeat after me:
It is not my place
to tell Black people
how to protest.
It is my duty
to call out racism.

740.

Let's slowly drill in them
a sense of patriotism-
let's tell them that *they are*
the national anthem,
the flag, and other symbolism.
So that when they grow up to see
our injustice and cruelty,
fighting us will unleash an inner war
that feels like a betrayal
to who *they are*.

***

Home
is inside me.

Home
is not this land
that doesn't understand
my needs
my rights.

They say
home is where the heart is.
I say
my only home is my heart.

741.

We're brainwashed
to believe
the police
protect us,
by the people
who fund
the police
to kill us.

***

Saying:

**"He shouldn't have resisted the police,
that's why he got shot"**

is as ridiculous as saying:

**"She shouldn't have resisted the sexual advances,
that's why she got raped"**

And it's equally ridiculous to suggest
that complying with a police arrest
and complying with a rapist,
is a guarantee
that you won't get hurt.

N.B. George Floyd didn't resist arrest while he was begging police to let him breathe for 8 minutes and 46 seconds. Stop victim blaming. Defund the fucking police.

742.

When I was 10
I was terrified of police
because they carry a gun.
But my father told me
that they do it to protect us
not to hurt anyone.

When I was 15
my mom called the cops
for help during a traffic dispute.
And while she talked with one
the other one told me I was cute.
He slipped his phone number
into my palm.
I took it quietly because I was scared
of his firearm.

When I was 20
I've learned that to get out of any street trouble in peace
I must force myself to smile and flirt with the police,
even if I was reporting to them an incident of abuse
I must make myself open to their advances if they so choose.

What I'm trying to say is
my 10 year old instinct
was right-
those who carry a gun
don't necessarily use it to protect,

but to get away with
abusing anyone.

N.B. www.mappingpoliceviolence.org

743.

I can't read to my son
any bedtime stories.

I can't read to him the story
about the cops who save the day,
because in real life cops are just criminals
licensed to take lives away.

I can't read to him the story
about how everyone plays fair,
because in real life
your skin colour cuts your share.

I can't read to him any of the stories
that my mother read to me,
about all the good in this world
distorting my reality.

So when he asks me to read a bedtime story
I tell him we are the story
and the scattered stars in the sky
are watching us, to learn how to unite;
and instead of reading anything to him, I just hold him,
and kiss him, goodnight.

744.

When you see your fellow
human being
suffering
due to oppression on their race,
and you do absolutely nothing
to make the world a better place,
justifying by saying:
"...but it's not my problem..."

You are the problem.

And if you get offended
when asked to check
your privilege
because
you're not part of the problem...

Newsflash:
You ARE the problem.

745.

All White people
are born in a system
of privilege.
In that matter, they have no choice.
But they have the liberty to decide
how to use their voice.

All rich people
are born in a system
of privilege.
In that matter, they have no choice.
But they have the liberty to decide
how to use their voice.

All able-bodied people
are born in a system
of privilege.
In that matter, they have no choice.
But they have the liberty to decide
how to use their voice.

All heterosexuals
are born in a system
of privilege.
In that matter, they have no choice.

But they have the liberty to decide
how to use their voice.

All cis people
are born in a system
of privilege.
In that matter, they have no choice.
But they have the liberty to decide
how to use their voice.

All men
are born in a system
of privilege.
In that matter, they have no choice.
But they have the liberty to decide
how to use their voice.

All *human* beings
are born in a system
of privilege.
In that matter, they have no choice.
But they have the liberty to decide
how to use their voice.

N.B. "Not all" is a silencing strategy that redirects the focus away

from the oppressed to oppressor again. Instead of saying "not all",
check your privilege and use your voice wisely. Remember: privilege
is not just White, it comes in many forms. Unless we ALL check ALL
forms of privilege we carry how can we hope to do better for the most
oppressed of us?

746.

To understand your privilege,
don't look at the things you can't do-
look at the things you can do.

To understand your oppression,
don't look at the things you can do-
look at the things you can't do.

747.

The only situation
wherein
it is acceptable to treat
Whites and Colours
separately,
is when you are doing
your laundry.

748.

After the media dies down
and the protestors end their rally,
here's a simple way to remember
how to continue being an ally:

Each time you take a breath
for granted
(because there is no reason
that you shouldn't)-
remember George Floyd
and the countless Black lives
who couldn't.

                              ***

And a month later...
a year later...
a lifetime later...

As we're teaching our children
their role in dismantling
systemic racism and oppression-
remember,
this hierarchal food-chain
of supremacy and suppression;

A White man
was called as a saviour by an Arab man
and obediently shielded by an Asian man,

as he murdered
a Black man
who called for
his "Mama".

N.B. The women always come last.

749.

I weep.

For Black women.
For trans women.

I weep.

For different shades of skin.
For different gender orientations.

I weep.

For women who have everything to lose
over nothing they got to choose.

I weep.

And I realize
it is privilege
that I just get to weep-
when there are women who keep their eyes peeled
because they're terrified of even
going to sleep.

N.B. Breonna Taylor, a Black woman from Kentucky U.S.A. was
sleeping when she was shot to death by White cops who busted into
the wrong home looking for a drug dealer. Maha Almutairi, a trans
woman from Kuwait, was sentenced to a men's jail for the "crime" of

being trans in an Arab country. She released a video (https://youtu.be/yJ1mZB_pmB4) which went viral- in it she says she was raped and sexually assaulted in jail, even while she was asleep. TWO HORRIFIC INCIDENTS HAPPENED ONLY MONTHS APART IN TWO DIFFERENT PARTS OF THE WORLD.

750.

I've fallen in love
with so many women
whom I've fantasized
about touching their bodies
the way they've touched my heart.

I've had desires
rip through me like the Amazon fire,
and tear my breath
apart.

And the only way
I can reach orgasm,
is for me to just write
about my passion
for those women...

For another me, in another lifetime.

For now I'm trapped in a body, in a country
where homosexuality
is a punishable crime.

N.B. The Arab world is unapologetically homophobic. I dream of
seeing change in my lifetime.

751.

To this cruel world:
Don't ever forget
the woman
who pinned the rainbow
into the dark sky.
You get to live
with your cruelty,
but her pride
will never die.

Rest in Pride Sarah Hegazi.

N.B. Sarah Hegazi was an Egyptian LGBTQI+ activist who was
imprisoned for holding up the rainbow flag in a concert in Egypt. In
jail she was humiliated and abused. After jail, she sought asylum in
Canada. She died by suicide while in Canada, at age 30, after
struggling to get over her traumatic experience.

752.

Don't tell queer people they deserve to live-
they know that already.
Ask your non-queer people
why they don't know that already?

***

Follow Queer communities online.
Follow Black, Indigenous, and People of Colour.
Follow the voices you've never heard.

Social media is a classroom;
and it's the biggest one in the world.

753.

My only son is three.
He loves cars
and playing Barbie.
He pretends to be
an astronaut
on a pretend mission,
then he pretends to cook
with his pretend kitchen.
He loves glitter, and stories,
and puzzles, and dinosaurs.
He sensibly has no sense
of gender discourse.

***

Perhaps, we're all queer.

Observe the innocence of children
as they cross-dress in role play,
observe their lack of gendering
before you teach them how to say
'right' vs. 'wrong',
before you draw boxes for them
to 'naturally' belong.

Perhaps, we're all queer.

Some of us decide to sit
inside those socially constructed norms.

Some of us decide to bravely walk
the long journey back home.

754.

My child
has the choice
to be sexual or to be asexual
to be queer or to be straight.

The only choice
I have as a parent
is to arm my child
with the love they need
to liberate,
from a world
imprisoned
by hate.

***

Disowning your child
because they have
a different sexual orientation
than you,
is like
disowning your child
because their favourite colour is yellow
while yours is blue.

***

Why does it matter
what your child's
sexual orientation is?
You're not the one
they'll be having
sex with!

755.

They say being gay is *unnatural*
because it can't produce children.

Do you know why they say that?

Do you know why
they shame women for choosing to get abortions
or being child-free?

It has nothing to do with defying "nature"-
it is about defying the "nature" of a capitalist economy.

If you're not producing children (future consumers and labourers)-
how can the rich continue to be?!

***

You know why they criminalize
being gay and queer
and getting abortions
and free speech?

Because when those people are put in jail
they can't vote.

And when they can't vote
there is no hope

for the laws to change.

There is no hope
that gays and queers
and people with wombs
and free thinkers
will ever have a world
that represents them.

756.

I was 13
when I went to my first drag show
saw
my first Queen.
She was the most beautiful woman
my eyes had ever seen.

Her hair, her makeup
her dress, her legs,
her feminine
conformance.

She was the one
who first made me realize
that gender is a performance.

                                        ***

Imagine
if gender was a playground
and anyone can pick
any gender they want to play.

Slides or swings to sway.

Or even the sand-box.

Run around with your shoes
or barefoot without socks.

Imagine
if gender was a playground
and everyone was welcome inside-
your *sex* doesn't determine
what you can or cannot ride.

Imagine
how happy everyone would be on that playground
where it is clearly understood,
that the only rule
is for everyone to feel good.

Imagine.

Imagine
if gender was a playground...
because that's what it
actually is.

***

Gender is a performance
of a script written by society
casting roles to our genitals
without allowing us to audition.

Burn that script.

To perform-
you don't need a script or permission.

757.

We see the world
as black and white,
but what about grey?

We see the world
as morning and night,
but what about midday?

We see the world
as male and female
but what about intersex?

We see the world
as straight and gay
but what about bi-sex?

When we see the world
we simplify
what we see.

But the world is not
a binary.

***

Saying you can only be
male or female
man or woman
gay or straight

with no possibility
for anything in between-
is like saying
in the world there is only
pure good or pure evil
and nothing else in between.

N.B. Get out of your binary thinking mode!

758.

You know why
we live in a
binary
hetero-normative
world?

Because when
a baby is born
the doctors decided
to proclaim
"it's a boy!" or "it's a girl!"

And then they wash out
the remnants from womb
(which are red)-
and place the newborn accordingly
in a blue or pink bed.

***

"BUT SEX IS BIOLOGICAL"
they yell at me
whenever I advocate for trans equality.

"Sure" I say,
"but you know what's not biological?
The socially constructed
language and tools,
that are used to create
said biological rules".

759.

Not everyone
with a womb
is a woman.

Not everyone
with a penis
is a man.

But everyone
is an asshole
if they won't understand-
that sex and gender
don't necessarily
go hand in hand.

N.B. www.humandignitytrust.org

760.

People often confuse:
Gender with **Sex**
and
Sex with **Binary**
and
Binary with **Biology**.

And this type of ignorance
literally kills
the queer community.

***

Gender is a socially created idea, which says that women should behave a certain way (e.g. wear dresses, shave their legs, tend to housework, etc) and men should behave in another (opposite) way (wear pants, have hairy legs, be breadwinner etc). Notice how people get upset if you mess up those gender divisions e.g. if a woman doesn't shave her legs, or if a man wears a dress. How do we assign people into women and men in the first place? We look at their Sex.

Sex is a biological idea that largely relies on what your genitals look like. If you are born with a vulva (your doctor assigns your sex as female, and society assigns your gender as girl then woman). If you are born with a penis (your doctor assigns your sex as male, and society assigns your gender as boy then man). So what's the problem then? The concept of Binary.

Binary means only two. When you are born and the doctor assigns you as either female or male- they are picking from one of two options. This has led us to erroneously believe that Sex must be Binary. In other words the only possible options for one's Sex is one of two (female or male). But this is an incomplete story. Research constantly shows that Sex is not a Binary but rather a continuum. On one far end there is female and on the other extreme there is male. While most of us fall on those extremes, there is a host of other options in the middle too that many people fall under. You could be intersex. Or you could be closer on the continuum to "female" physically, but your make-up is closer to "male" or vice versa. Because Sex isn't as simple as what your genitals look like- hormones and chromosomes also play a role and they aren't always clear-cut. Thus the possibilities of Sex are many. So what is the problem? The problem is that this truth doesn't sit well with people because it tells us that "Binary" is bullshit. But why do we want to hold on to the idea of Binary anyway?

Because we erroneously think that when it comes to Sex, Binary is **Biology**. How did we come to think that way? Back to when doctors often assign new-borns as either female or male- we think those are the only two options that exist because we believe doctors. We believe doctors because doctors rely on Biology. And Biology gives us facts. While it's true that Biology is factual- the problem is we think of facts as clear-cut and simple 2+2=4. You can't argue with that. But facts aren't that simple. 1+3=4 too, and 1.5 +2.5=4 as well, and (you get the idea). There are so many possibilities. Biology is not Binary. And because facts aren't so simple, even doctors MAKE MISTAKES of assigning the wrong sex for folks who do not clearly fall on the extreme ends of the Sex continuum.

To sum up:

-Gender doesn't have to fit a certain Sex (screw the man-made rules! This is what feminism fights to eradicate).

-Sex is a continuum not a Binary (and that's a fact!).

-Binary isn't the rule of Biology (it is much more complex than just two options).

N.B. Recommended reading: "Sex redefined" on www.nature.com and "Skeletal studies show sex, like gender, exists along a spectrum" on www.discovermagazine.com

761.

I am a woman.

So what if I was
assigned male
at birth?

Are you saying
that doctors
make no errors,
and that errors
have no worth?

I am evidence.

I am paying for the doctor's negligence,
with your hate.

But I am a woman.

And this is not a debate.

762.

Dear J.K. Rowling,

The word you are looking for is '*men*'.

Your problem is with *men*
(not with trans women).

You were assaulted by a *man*
(not a trans woman).

You want single-sex spaces
to protect women from *men*
(not from trans women).

You worry that women would be attacked
by *men* who pretend to be trans women
(not trans women).

Your fears and concerns are valid,
but they are to do with *men*
(not with trans women).

Your problem is with *men*
(specifically cis *men*).

Trans women are not *men*.

N.B. A response to J.K. Rowling's 10th June, 2020 essay titled "J.K. Rowling Writes about Her Reasons for Speaking out on Sex and Gender Issues". She wrote this piece after being criticized for taking issue with an article discussing menstruation products while using the phrase "people who menstruate". Rowling has tweeted in response to said article: "'People who menstruate.' I'm sure there used to be a word for those people. Someone help me out. Wumben? Wimpund? Woomud?"

Rowling has a consistent history with transphobia. There is no amount of essays one can write to justify bigotry.

763.

Dear Trans-exclusionary Radical Feminists;
To suggest that
trans women are not *real* women
and trans men are not *real* men-
is to suggest that gender is *'real'*
instead of an arbitrary social construct.

And if you believe gender is 'real'
then why are you fighting to dismantle
gender stereotyping upheld by patriarchy?

                              ***

I don't understand
trans-exclusionary radical feminists.

Seriously,
what's your problem?
That someone is saying they've *transitioned* into a gender?

Gender isn't an innate biological structure
we all transition into gender!

Gender is arbitrarily linked to sex.
There is natural law to it
no logic, no common sense.

If you believe
gender is innate to sex

then why are you even a feminist?
What are you trying to abolish?

The premise of feminism is to fight for equality-
the idea that gender is innate to sex
is the premise upheld by patriarchy,
and it is the main cause of inequality.

Why call it
trans-exclusionary radical feminism
when it's clearly
trans-exclusionary radical bigotry?

                            ***

According to
trans-exclusionary radical feminists
trans women should be excluded from feminism because they *had* the
privilege of being boys/men.

Following that logic;
Cis women should be excluded from feminism because they *have* the
privilege of being cis.

And why stop there?
White women should be excluded from feminism because they *have*
the privilege of being White.
And straight women should be excluded, able-bodied women, rich
women, beautiful women, thin women...

You know what?

ALL WOMEN should be excluded from feminism because they *have* the privilege (over animals) of being human!

Feminism is about dismantling privilege.
Being included in feminism shouldn't be a privilege.

***

Feminism must include trans women.

It doesn't matter that they had the privileges a male would;
what matters is that they experience
the oppressions of womanhood.

764.

Femininity is softness.
Feminism is assertiveness.

You don't have to pick either/or.
You can be both in one.
You can be some.
You can be more...

***

Yes, I'm a feminist
and I still wear lipstick
and cute dresses.

Because
my fight isn't against
feminine expression,
my fight is against
women's oppression.

765.

We expect women's bodies
to become feminine,
yet to have feminine bodies
we're not expected
to become women.

I can't live in a girl's body forever.

***

I was taught
that to be accepted
I must take less space-
that in this world
women must *shrink*
to fit into place.

So I began to suck
my belly in,
shave the hairs poking
out of my skin

Constantly creating a *smaller* version,
of me.
Until she became
my reality.

I swallowed

my voice,
I stripped off
my choice.

That was my invoice.

I was a girl with the accountability of a woman,
and a woman who must look like a girl.

Hiding in my shell, like a precious pearl.

Each time I dared
to stand taller,
they pushed me
to stay smaller
and that's when I began
to truly understand-
what Alice had to give up
to be in Wonderland.

N.B. I will not shrink, fuck what you taught me to think- and fuck
your Wonderland.

766.

Irina Dunn
famously said
"a woman without a man
is like a fish without a bicycle".

I'd like to agree
but I find that too radical.

Women need men.

Women need men
because who else can we
ask to open jars?

Women need men
because who can protect us
when we're travelling
or going to bars?

Women need men.

Women need men
because who else will explain
how our bodies work to us?
And what's best for us?
And if we dare, to think for ourselves,
who will make a fuss?

Women need men
and not just on a whim.

Women need men
because a fish needs a bicycle
when all her life
she's been told she can't swim.

767.

Women have yet to attain full victory.
Remnants live on
from our oppressive history.

Women are now allowed to vote
but no one votes for us.
And for whom to vote
the men in our lives pressure us.

Women are now allowed to work
outside the house.
But childcare and housework are still jobs
not shared with our spouse.

Women are now allowed to own
a bank account and property.
But we are not paid for the same work
that men do, equally.

Women are now allowed to escape
a fate of motherhood.
But we are shamed for abortions
although sperms contribute.

Women are now allowed to live
without depending on a man.
But if we do we are cussed
as spinster and lesbian.

Women are now allowed to speak
and write freely about our oppression

without being considered trouble-makers.
But if we do we are labelled
as man-haters.

Women have yet to attain any victory.
Remnants not only live on, they're constantly re-born, ingrown
from our collective misery.

***

The most dangerous
strategy of oppression
is the one that tells victims
they have a 'choice',
yet there are no safe structures
for their expression
of an alternative voice.

Want to take off your hijab? It's your choice!
But if I do, I'm condemned endlessly.

Want to leave your abusive husband? It's your choice!
But I've been trained that women can't survive independently.

Want to travel alone? It's your choice!
But then I'm seen as an easy target consequently.

This fucked up strategy
not only
induces
victim shame-

but those who struggle to make a 'choice'
think it's their fault, and they resort
to self-blame.

768.

As a woman
(and specifically a Brown woman)
I've been implicitly and explicitly taught
that I should be grateful.

Grateful that I got to go to school
when my grandmother couldn't.
Grateful that I got to go to grad school
when my mother didn't.

Grateful.

Grateful that I can vote, get a job,
my own bank account, and own property.
Grateful that my husband is a liberal
who doesn't believe in oppressing me.

Grateful.

Grateful that I can take off my hijab
or wear a short dress.
Grateful that people are listening when I say I'm still oppressed.

Grateful.

It's as if my hard work isn't a part of the equation-
it's as if I didn't have to fight to continue my education
as if I don't continue to battle everyday discrimination
as if I didn't endure war to marry a man who isn't from my bloodline
as if I didn't spend years unlearning that my body isn't mine
and as if sharing this knowledge doesn't take energy and time...

As if I'm not great...

I'm not grateful.

I'm great-full.

And all that you want me to be grateful for
is actually- my right.

***

You know what's
the ultimate tragedy?

I still have to fight
to take the rights
that the women before me
already secured for me,
because the mindsets of misogyny
haven't changed.

769.

Each morning
I take a moment
to mourn
myself.

My freedom was snatched
from the second I hatched
out of my mother's
womb.

It's true I'm living and I'm writing
but I'm doing it from inside my
tomb.

***

They train us to be silent
through gifts
then threats
then prisons
then guns.

They allow us
to be seen
but not heard.

Because they know
that our tongues,
are the most dangerous weapons
in the whole wide world.

770.

Do you notice the ways you're silenced
from speaking out?

Your oppressors don't just silence you
when they scream and shout.

They silence you when they call you names-
crazy, man-hater, idiot
it's all the same.

They silence you when they slut-shame
if you decide to have sex
or take off your hijab,
yet they'll call you a prude or ugly
if you won't let them grab
your pussy-
don't you see?
You can't win whichever way
there is no logic to the way
they silence you.

It is all an attempt to control you.

And when you call them out,
on their bullshit
they shout;
"Not all men behave the same way!"
Yet, "not all" is just another silencing strategy
that redirects the focus away
from the oppressed to oppressor again.

It's all the same.

Do you notice the ways you're silenced?

You have the right **to not remain silent**, when they do that again.
Don't let them win, and go do this
to other women.

Keep speaking
like iron, don't get deterred.

What you have to say is important
and it's your right to be heard.

771.

When are women and other oppressed minorities silenced?

When they speak/express/take space in a world unaccustomed to holding space for them.

What are the silencing strategies?

The silencing strategies are just the word 'shut up' dressed up in different outfits. Those outfits include (but not limited to): insults, bullying, trolling, discrimination, threats, gaslighting, being ignored, not being believed, being interrupted, and even physical violence.

How do the silencing strategies work?

They induce a negative reaction in the victim (sadness/anger/guilt/shame/fear/etc.) that becomes psychologically linked with their speaking/expressing/taking space. Overtime, to avoid experiencing those negative reactions, the victim will remain silent. The oppressor thus achieves their goal.

How can you dismantle the power of silencing strategies?

1- Recognize the types of silencing strategies and realize they are a way of saying 'shut up'.

2-Unlearn your negative reaction so that the silencing strategies lose their power over you (hard but not impossible once you are aware of the strategies).

3- Continue speaking/expressing/taking space and remember it is healthy to cut out toxic people/environments that stop you from being you!

772.

Whenever they want to shame me
they make up names to call me.

Slut: simply because I enjoy having sex.
Prude: because I said 'no' when they wanted me to say 'yes'.
Whore: because I charge money, for what they want to get for free.
Crazy: because I call them out, when they gaslight me.
Dyke: because I love women, and this presents competition that
threatens heterosexual men.

This is what it comes down to;
a woman is shamed for exercising
the same rights that men do.

Take a moment to reflect;
what is the real meaning
behind the slurs they hurl, at you?

N.B. Cyber aggression targets women on a daily basis. A study finds
that 2.9 million tweets in one week contain instances of gendered
insults e.g. bitch, cunt, slut, or whore. (Source: Felmlee D., Inara
Rodis P., & Zhang A. (2020), "Sexist slurs: Reinforcing feminine
stereotypes online", Sex Roles, Vol. 83, pp. 16-28).

773.

Too revealed.
Too modest.
Too bold.
Too shy.

Too bossy.
Too pushy.
Too confident.
Too sly.

Too much.
Too little.
No matter how much or how little
you try.

Have you ever
wondered why,
they label you
as a "too"?

It is just something they say
when you stray away
from the path
they're pushing you to.

Too.

***

I am not responsible
for the way I am constructed
in the male gaze.

They see me as a whore,
so they shame me for it.

They see me as a prude,
so they make fun of me for it.

I am not responsible
for what men see.

The only construction
I accept for myself
is the one I create
for me.

774.

Speak.

Speak from the line of ancestors
of which you were born,
speak for the children of your womb
who aren't yet home.

Speak.

For what is immortal
other than a voice?

***

We don't only
pass recipes
down the maternal lineage-
we also pass down
wounds and pain,
guilt and shame,
and silence
and resilience
and power
and wishes
and hopes
and dreams.

We are much more than
pies and cookies and creams.

775.

I've inherited
my mother's skin
and her eyes
and her wounds
and her resilience.

But I refuse
to inherit
her silence.

***

Silence
is a trait
inherited
by generations
of women.

You can't turn back time.

But remember
that your silence too
will be passed down
your ancestral line.

Break the chain.

776.

Long after I'm gone
and my bones
turn into dust
again...
What will be left
other than those pages
telling you about
my joy and my pain?

***

Tonight
I whispered a fable
into my son's ears-
a lullaby with a rhyme from my heartbeats
for his coming years.

Tonight
I told my 3 year old
a bedtime story
about a Mommy on a mission
to save the world.
She waves her magic pen to write
when everyone is asleep at night,
except for the stars-
she sits with them, with her cup of tea
and they tell her the same story
about play pretend,
about shooting stars dressed as fireflies

and fireflies dressed as shooting stars,
about bravery dressed as courage
and courage dressed as bravery,
about oceans dressed as the sea
and....

I stop talking
to check if my son is already sleepy-
but he asks, with bright twinkles in his eyes,
"Mommy,
is this story about you and me?"

777.

My strengths, because I am a woman,
are seen as weaknesses.

My life, because I am a woman,
is seen as only fit for marriage.

But I am not someone's daughter
in transit to be someone's wife.

And I've noticed, because I am a woman,
when I say I'm fearless
when I say I want to choose what to do with my body and my life,
they try to shun me because
they're threatened by me.
They're afraid of losing their grip on me
so they try and try to shame me
to break me
it's easier to control a broken person.

When I say I'm fearless, because I am a woman,
the world becomes afraid of me.

Let them be.

I'd rather live feared
than live afraid.

                              ***

I sought refuge in feminism,
from a world that is created by

yet strikingly hates
women.

I am shredding shame
from my skin.
And I cannot begin to explain,
the pain I'm in.

I used to think shame was
such a beautiful dress-
I wore it proudly, to impress
until I realized
my entire life has become a mess-
for I've grown out of that dress
in that size, that style
but I squeezed myself in it, to make others smile.

I lost my smile.

I lost my smile
as shame
became
my second skin.
And now, it's not so simple to undress.

Now I have to shred shame
drip out of blood and pain,
because you can't just strip off what's been suppressed.
But I'm doing it because I don't want to wear shame-
my style's changed
and I want to wear
women's progress.

778.

I am not
my oppression.

I am a revolution
dressed in skin.

You're a fool
when you say
I won't live
to see the day,
when women are free...

I took this torch
from the woman before me,
and I am lighting up the porch
for the woman after me.

There is no destination.
This is a journey.

***

Dear Girls and Women,

You can be
whoever you want to be.

You can be magic
(because you are magic).

You can be fire
(because you are fire).

You can be the Eden
of whatever you desire.

Open the door, walk the path,
lead.

This world is but treading,
under your feet.

May we open this dark path...
and may women lead with their fire to light the way.

779.

I have met so many people in this life
who, like me,
are wandering;
from school to school
from job to job
from country to country,
from the day they are born.

Perhaps, when we leave the womb
we never again find home.

***

I've brought home some souvenirs
from foreign lands;

-Women's rights to choice
-A broken CD of the *Backstreet Boys*
-A Mexican recipe, and Irish coffee
-A prayer book from Bali
-Handcrafts from Maldives
-Crunchy Maple leaves
-A Russian doll
-The concept of equality for all
-Heartbeats of an African dance
-The fragrance of an Italian romance
-Understanding LGBTQ rights to choose
-Five tattoos
-Hundreds of books, thousands of conversations

-Countless realizations

I've brought home some souvenirs
from foreign lands.
They tell you the world is so big
but I'll tell you it can fit
right into your hands.

780.

I broke those rusty bronze shackles
that I inherited from my grandmother
who left them for me, thinking they were jewellery
locked around my wrists
like *Cartier* Love bracelets.

I broke those rusty bronze shackles
and then-
I wrote my story,
all over again.

***

I write about surviving
because I've survived
through writing.

***

Poetry
is a political prisoner
of art.
And bailing it
liberates
the heart.

781.

My mother
has a distrust
of medicine,
so growing up
I had to find
alternatives for healing-
art, poetry, and music
were the painkillers
to the hurt I was feeling.

***

A fresh stalk of mint leaves,
is stalking my black tea.
Reminds me of my mother's recipe:
for headaches, for heartbreaks
add mint, to lessen
the pain of the lesson
and stop swallowing Western medicine.

Around the greens,
I twiddle my thumbs
rip them from their roots,
till they go numb.

Perhaps now,
it's safe to dip them in
my black tea.

Perhaps now,
they won't feel their tender skin
scalding under my mercy.

I sip my tea,
and a childhood memory
comes sinking back.
Oh Mother, those mint leaves felt the burn-
they have all turned black.

782.

Dear Future Daughter,

I'm writing this
because they jailed
my tongue in my mouth
and locked my lips
so I won't speak.
But I want you to know that
your mother
was never
weak.

N.B. If silence was words...you'd realize I never stopped speaking.

783.

I use a pen name when I write,
because I didn't choose the name I was given-
I didn't choose this oppression
born swaddled with suppression.

I use a pen name when I write,
because I didn't choose the name I was given-
I didn't choose for my fate to be fatal in family honour,
needing permission, for my self-expression
like the lineage of women in my succession.

I use a pen name when I write,
because I chose this name
like I chose to be this woman-
I chose to gallop on this fierce pen,
I chose to whistle with the waves of the winds
that blew away
my veil,
my family's honour,
my name-
the one stamped on my I.D. with ink
inkling of shame;
"Name: [*insert woman's name*]",
"Sex: *Female*",
"Nationality: *Family honour*".

I am done being treated as
daughter, sister, wife, mother.

My given name is the name of a woman,
but my pen name is the name of all women.

I use a pen name when I write,
because I chose this name for myself.
And from now on,
when it comes to my life, I will choose everything else.

***

I look in the mirror
to look at her...

Hello, *Me*-
yup, that's my name
from now on,
my name isn't the one
written on my birth certificate
chosen by my parents
based on what girls are named-
no,
that's not my name. I am not
playing that game. Carrying honour and shame-
no.

From now on, my name is
Me
and I follow no one's expectations
on who
I must be.

784.

They told me drinking is a sin-
so I got drunk on stars.

They told me sex is a sin-
so I made love out of wars.

They told me being a lesbian is a sin-
so I fell in love with the woman,
that is me.

And each time they recount a sin-
I embrace it within,
my sense of morality.

785.

They tell me:
Be careful
with all this feminism you spew-
it intimidates and turns off men
they don't like this type of woman,
don't come crying if no one marries you.

I tell them:
What about me?
In your world do I get to have a preference
on the type of man I'd like to marry?
If he isn't actively dismantling
patriarchy,
privilege,
toxic masculinity,
and even the Lord-
I don't desire him
to dismantle
my headboard.

***

You know what's sexier
than a man
working on
his abs?
A man
working on

his inner healing.

I state this without any sarcasm;
if your unresolved shit
is as big
as your 'monstrous' dick-
it's the reason why
I can't orgasm.

786.

...And despite all the
upheld patriarchy
systematic misogyny
structural sexism
oppressive inequality...
I *still*
make love
to men...

Perhaps
we each
can only speak
in the language
we've been taught.

787.

"You're doing a great job" my father tells me.

I am shocked.

"But I am rebelling against patriarchy,
I am rebelling against everything you taught me,
I am walking on a lonely path
disdained by everyone at our home".

He smiles and says,
"yes. But you're doing a great job
at showing all the rebels
that they aren't walking alone".

***

Re-interpretation of *If You're Happy and You Know It*:

If you're a feminist and you know it-
clap your hands!

If you're a feminist and you know it-
clap your hands!

If you're a feminist and you know it,
then you know it takes two hands to *equally* show it...

If you're a feminist and you know it-
clap your hands!

788.

I have spent
so many nights
curled up
in the laps
of books,
pressing my fingertips
against their spines.
I have touched pages
that felt like skin
pulsating into mine.

I have lovers
resting on the shelves of libraries-
lovers who broke my heart
lovers who tore me apart
lovers that I begged to stay
lovers who won't go away,
staying up all night
until the dawn of the next day.
Lovers that just want to pick up a fight,
lovers that used fire to light
up my soul-
the number of lovers I have in libraries
is out of control.

And I still desire more,
perhaps I am what you think I am-
yes, I am a book whore.

789.

I will talk about sex.
I will write about sex.

Don't tell me it's a taboo
to utter what happens
between me and you.

I am not ashamed of my sins
I am not ashamed of this whiskey skin
I am not ashamed of the maze of pink that sink
between my thighs.
I am not ashamed of getting lost in pleasure, getting you lost in
pleasure.
I am not ashamed of the flutter
shutter
of butterflies
pulsating in the meadow
of the spring
of my groin.

I am not ashamed of the folds and flaps
that hold you deep
rooted
grounded
into a restful sleep.

I am not ashamed of all the joys my body
can give
me and you.
I am not ashamed, but tell me darling,
why are you?

790.

"Be yourself"

I was told.

By the books I loved as a child
by the movies on TV
by my mother.

I thought it was easy to be myself,
because how could one
be anything other?

And over the years
I slowly morphed
from caterpillar to butterfly,
from ugly duckling to a swan.
Who am I?
I stopped
when I became the black sheep.

Sometimes, to "be yourself"
you don't have to
take
any leap.

There are different versions of being yourself. Are you just being the
version society accepts?

791.

Once upon a time,
in a not so far away patriarchal land-
misogyny and bullshit
was getting out of hand.

All the girls and women
got together, to braid their own plaits
and paint their own fingernails-
and then they began the excruciating process
of re-telling their fairytales.

That "happily ever after"
certainly rings true-
but they tell the stories
from a man's point of view.

For girls and women are not made
to make themselves pretty, and then to get laid,
or to wait for prince charming to sweep
them off their feet,
so that they spend their lifetime
sweeping his castle,
and planting his seed
deep in their belly
to make a baby...

Because what if, possibly, maybe...

Girls and women had other dreams
besides staying at home-
what if girls and women were given the chance

to not dream of romance,
what would the world look like
if girls and women decide to fight
for a happy ending that isn't about men
that doesn't include marrying them...?

Let's re-imagine
that "Once upon a time"-
only it ends with a woman's victory
this time.

***

Once upon a time,
in a not so far away patriarchal land-
misogyny and bullshit
was getting out of hand.

The princess woke up one day
decided she will no longer stay
in her parents' castle, waiting for prince charming.

The entire kingdom found this alarming.

But she packed up her shit
told her parents that's it,
and gave everyone her goodbyes.

For she doesn't want to *rule* this world
she wants to *live* in this world,
and experience *everything*

before she dies.

N.B. Re-write your fucking fairytale!

792.

Women are viewed as frightening when they have power.

In fairytales
there's always
a wicked witch
an evil stepsister
and a cruel stepmother.

Have you noticed
how it's so significantly rare
to find a wicked, evil, cruel
male character?

***

Imagine this:

The prince turns into a frog.
And the princess turns into a whore.

How much more
fun would that fairytale be?

793.

To the girl who became a woman
that cannot choose between
being a princess, or being a whore;
you can be both...
...because you're so much more!

***

You're a whore!
they say,
when I try to peak through the door
they kept me behind
firmly shut.

You want to take off your hijab?
You must be a slut!

You want a boyfriend, or ten?
Don't see romance as a means to an end?
Or worse, you're a lesbian?!
Now you want us to be okay, with you having a girlfriend?

You're a whore!

But you know what?
If going after what I want
makes me a whore,
I'd rather be a whore
than miss out
on so much more

in life.

I'd rather dress how I want, call me a slut
I'd rather choose my husband or wife.

You want me to be a princess
in some virginal fairytale land,
but here's what you don't understand...
you can't program my desires like a machine,
I'd rather be the queen
of the entire fucking *whore-istan*!

***

Whore, slut, bitch, cunt,
stupid, crazy, man-hater,
you deserve to die.

People ask me
how do you deal
with those insults
all the time?

I tell them
it takes rotten grapes
to make fine wine.

794.

Who the fuck
do you think
you are?

All billions of us
are just dust
that burst
out of the same star.

***

For what is
the black sheep
the odd one out
the outcast
the weirdo,
other than someone
breaking the norms
you're used to?

For what is
the black sheep
the odd one out
the outcast
the weirdo,
other than someone
questioning the norms
you've unquestionably accepted?

I'd rather be the black sheep, than a sheep.

I'd rather be the odd one out, than question my own doubt.

I'd rather be the outcast, than let my morals come last.

I'd rather be the weirdo, than a finger puppet at your show.

I'd rather be authentically me, than a version filtered by society.

795.

Why do you choose to believe them?

When they tell you
you are stupid, you are ugly, you are worthless...

Why do you choose to believe them?

You can't control what they say
you can't even choose what they say,
but *believing them is a choice.*

And it's always your choice.

796.

When you hurt your body
it will hurt you back.

When you don't sleep
it will be tired.

When all you eat
is junk food
and all you drink is whiskey
and all you breathe are cigarettes
how can your body give you back
anything other than stress?

Your body merely reacts
to what you give it
what you feed it.

Choose better. Live better.

                              ***

You trust your lungs
to take the next breath
while you sleep.

You trust your legs
to take the next step
that you won't trip

over your feet.

You buy one ice cream
because you trust your hands
won't let it fall
before you eat.

From this place of blind trust,
take your next leap.

For you can only imagine
what you can actually
achieve.

Believe.

797.

What if I told you
that in fairytales;
the fairies, the wizards
and that magic spell song-
are actually symbolic
of the privileges
in which the characters belong?

***

Definition of *lucky*: A person with some sort of privilege, and who
knows how to use it.

798.

Being White doesn't mean you don't experience any hardships,
it means any hardships you experience
aren't to do with your skin colour.

Being rich doesn't mean you don't experience any hardships,
it means any hardships you experience
aren't to do with your financial status.

Being able-bodied doesn't mean you don't experience any hardships,
it means any hardships you experience
aren't to do with your body.

Being heterosexual doesn't mean you don't experience any hardships,
it means any hardships you experience
aren't to do with your sexual orientation.

Being cis doesn't mean you don't experience any hardships,
it means any hardships you experience
aren't to do with your gender expression.

Being a man doesn't mean you don't experience any hardships,
it means any hardships you experience
aren't to do with your gender.

***

Being Black doesn't mean you don't have any privileges,
it means any privileges you have
aren't to do with your skin colour.

Being poor doesn't mean you don't have any privileges,
it means any privileges you have
aren't to do with your financial status.

Being disabled doesn't mean you don't have any privileges,
it means any privileges you have
aren't to do with your body.

Being homosexual doesn't mean you don't have any privileges,
it means any privileges you have
aren't to do with your sexual orientation.

Being trans doesn't mean you don't have any privileges,
it means any privileges you have
aren't to do with your gender expression.

Being a woman doesn't mean you don't have any privileges,
it means any privileges you have
aren't to do with your gender.

799.

The revolution
starts with your thoughts...
But if it stays there,
it stops there!

For fuck's sake, do something!

How can you change the world?

Do something.

Something
is better than nothing.

Take action.
If you can't take action-
Speak.
If you can't speak-
Listen.
If you can't listen-
don't just look...

The world looks that way because we just look.

Do something!
Do anything!

Something
is better than nothing!

800.

"I'm a feminist, but..."
"I'm not a racist, but..."
"I'm pro-choice, but..."
"I'm an ally, but..."

Believe it or not-
you lost me
at 'but'.

Nothing good ever comes
out of a butt.

To the one holding fire:
Light up...

Light up all the shit!

Made in the USA
Columbia, SC
15 September 2024

41840926R00188